AN INTRODUCTION TO BIBLE GEOGRAPHY

AN INTRODUCTION
TO
BIBLE
GEOGRAPHY

by

Howard F. Vos

MOODY PRESS
CHICAGO

Library of Congress Cataloging in Publication Data

Vos, Howard Frederic, 1925-
An introduction to Bible geography.

Rev. ed. of: Beginnings in Bible geography.
Bibliography: p. 119
1. Bible—Geography.   I. Vos, Howard Frederic,
1925-   .   Beginnings in Bible geography.   II. Title.
BS630.V67   1983   220.9′1   83-17417
ISBN: 0-8024-0326-3

1 2 3 4 5 6 7 Printing/EB/Year 87 86 85 84 83

Printed in the United States of America

Contents

A Beginning Word

The biblical drama was acted out on the stage of geography. Just as stage props help to put an audience in the right mood for watching a play, promoting their understanding of it or becoming an integral part of the drama's presentation, so a knowledge of biblical geography is essential to an appreciation of the biblical story.

Ordinarily, a Bible student will look at Scripture from the viewpoint of his own geographical context. If he lives in the American Midwest, for example, he might visualize the story of Ruth as taking place in the wide expanse of a Nebraska wheatfield, rather than in the small valleys around Bethlehem. If his home is the bayou area of Louisiana, he might conclude that the Bible lands are hot, humid, and blessed with abundant rainfall, rather than understanding that places like Babylon, Beersheba, and Cairo enjoy less than ten inches of rainfall per year. If the student comes from the mountains of Kentucky or Tennessee, he might think of the Bible lands as generally hilly, rather than viewing some of them as generally flat, as in the case of Mesopotamia or the delta of Egypt. The Bible student needs to know about Bible geography in order to understand each narrative in its proper setting.

It is common for Bible students to recognize only one Bible land—Palestine. But if one follows present political divisions, he will have to expand his horizons to take in twelve Bible lands.

As the biblical story begins, the spotlight focuses on Mesopotamia (1) (modern Iraq), where civilization dawned, and where Abraham *Iraq*

7

launched the patriarchal period. Following the leading of God, Abraham moved to Canaan, or Palestine (currently Israel and Jordan); there the whole patriarchal narrative took place, with the exception of brief interludes in Egypt.

During a period of famine, Jacob and his family moved to Egypt, at the invitation of Pharaoh—prompted by Joseph. There the Hebrews were later enslaved and eventually managed to escape. After forty years of wandering in the Sinai and adjacent territory, they conquered much of Canaan and settled down there during the periods of the Judges, the United Kingdom, and the Divided Kingdom.

In the days of David and Solomon, Phoenicia[1] (modern Lebanon) was closely associated with the Hebrews. And during the divided monarchy, Syria became entangled in Israelite affairs. When the Northern Kingdom fell to Assyria in 723-722 B.C. and the Southern Kingdom to Babylon in 586 B.C., the spotlight again turned to Mesopotamia. After Persian conquest of the Babylonians, Iran provided the stage for such dramatic events as the story of Esther. Persians controlled the Near East at the close of the Old Testament.

In the early part of New Testament times, Palestine again came into the limelight, during the early ministry of Christ. Syria figured prominently in the conversion of the apostle Paul. When Paul began his ministry, he went first to Cyprus (now a sovereign republic) and then preached extensively in Asia Minor (modern Turkey) on his first and third missionary journeys and briefly on his second journey. On this journey, he spent close to two years in Greece. At the end of his third journey, Paul was imprisoned in Jerusalem and Caesarea and ultimately appealed to Caesar to adjudicate his case. On the way to Rome, he was shipwrecked on Melita, or Malta (now a sovereign state), spent three months there, and finally reached Italy and Rome, where he was imprisoned for two years.

Although the New Testament contains hints of later ministries of Paul, Peter, John, and others, there is no biblical account of ministry in additional geographical areas. Given that kind of limitation, the num-

---

1. Phoenicia (Tyre and Sidon) also bore the brunt of numerous prophecies of suffering and destruction, and Paul spent a week at Tyre (Acts 21:3-4).

ber of Bible lands may be said to stand at twelve.[2] In this book, Jordan and Israel are joined together in a single study on Palestine. So, although there are twelve Bible lands today if one counts sovereign states, there are eleven if one counts geographical regions.

The discussion of the geography of these lands in the following chapters occurs in the order of their appearances in the biblical narrative. The treatment is nontechnical and introductory. Those seeking a more detailed knowledge of specifics will find additional works listed at the end of the book.

---

2. Admittedly, the Queen of Sheba came from southern Arabia, Philip ministered to an Ethiopian eunuch, Simon of Cyrene in Libya carried the cross for Christ (see also Acts 2:10; 11:20; 13:1), and gold was periodically obtained from the land of Ophir (possibly in southern Arabia, East Africa, or India), but those references are fleeting and do not require geographical discussion for the Bible student to obtain perspective on the biblical narrative. Paul went out into Arabia after his conversion (Galatians 1:17), but that was probably somewhere fairly close to Damascus and thus within the territory of Syria. Paul mentioned plans to go to Spain (Romans 15:24), but the Bible does not relate his travels and ministry there. Crete figures in the biblical account, but it was not in New Testament times (and is not now) a sovereign state. Some discussion of the island appears in the chapter on Greece.

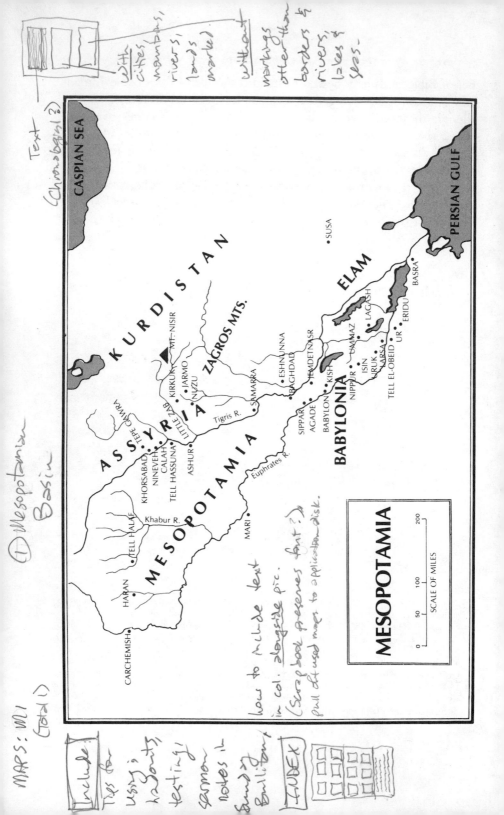

1

Mesopotamia

Civilization began in Mesopotamia and its environs. This is the assertion of the Bible, and modern scholarship agrees. In this general area the Garden of Eden was located. Noah's ark came to rest on the mountains of Ararat at the northern fringe of Mesopotamia. And after the Flood, descendants of Noah were involved in establishing such biblical cities as Erech, Nineveh, Calah, and Babylon in Mesopotamia (Genesis 10:10-11). Later on, Abraham was born in Ur—one of the greatest cities of the region. Subsequently, he moved to Haran in northern Mesopotamia. At Haran some of Abraham's relatives remained; there Abraham sought a wife for his son Isaac (Genesis 24); there Jacob married Leah and Rachel (Genesis 29); and there most of the progenitors of the twelve tribes of Israel were born.

Many centuries later, Assyria subjugated the kingdom of Israel and carried off thousands of Hebrews into captivity in Mesopotamia. Not long afterward, Babylon destroyed the kingdom of Judah and also carried off large numbers of Hebrews into Mesopotamia. There they remained until the Persians took over the area and permitted the Hebrews to go back home.

This area where so many biblical events took place is now encompassed by the state of Iraq, though Iraq is much larger than ancient Mesopotamia. Apparently the term *Mesopotamia*, meaning "land between the rivers," was coined by Jewish scholars in Alexandria, Egypt,

11

when they translated Genesis from Hebrew into Greek (the version called the Septuagint), probably during the third century B.C. The Mesopotamia reference in Genesis 24:10 translates the Hebrew, which literally means "Aram of the two rivers" and seems to apply to the small area between the Euphrates and the Khabur. But as translators of various versions have used the term, it has come to designate the region between the Euphrates and the Tigris. Greek historians and geographers of the second and first centuries B.C. used the term to apply to the area of Mesopotamia stretching north from the region of modern Baghdad. This is the equivalent of the territory which Arab geographers call *al Jazira* or *Gezirah* (the island); this area is roughly an island because the rivers come very close together near Baghdad. With the passage of time, the designation Mesopotamia has been extended to include the entire area between the Tigris and Euphrates, from the mountains of Armenia to the Persian Gulf; it even includes some land to the east and west of those great rivers. Roughly, the dimensions of the area may be put at 600 miles northwest to southeast and 300 miles from east to west.

Both the Tigris and Euphrates originate in the mountains of Armenia, less than 20 miles apart. The rivers flow in greatly divergent channels in a southeasterly direction until at one point they are 290 miles apart. Then they converge and near Baghdad flow about 25 miles apart. About 100 miles north of the Persian Gulf they join and spill their waters as one river (the Shatt-al-Arab) into the gulf.

The Tigris

The more eastern of the two rivers is the Tigris, called *Hiddekel* in the Old Testament (Genesis 2:14; Daniel 10:4). It rises on the southern slopes of the Taurus Mountains in present-day Turkey and cuts a bed 1,180 miles long on its way to the Persian Gulf. On its journey it is joined by several tributaries flowing from the mountains to the east: Khoser, Great Zab, Little Zab, Adhem, Diyala, and Duweirig. Although there is no evidence of any great change in the upper course of the Tigris, its lower course to the south of Baghdad was very unstable. During Old Testament times that part of the river flowed a considerable distance to the west of where it now is.

The Tigris floods annually. Its rise begins about the first of March; the waters reach their height in May and recede in June or July. At Baghdad the river is about a quarter of a mile wide, with a depth at high water of 26 feet and at low water of 4½ feet. The current in flood is about 4 miles per hour and at low water 1¼ miles per hour. The river is full of obstructions; the upper river is navigable only by native rafts; but from Baghdad approximately to a point where the Tigris joins the Euphrates, it is navigable by boats of some size.

Since the Tigris lies in a fairly deep bed, it was difficult for ancient peoples to raise its waters for irrigation as easily as they could those of the Euphrates. In fact, most of the course of the Tigris lies at a lower altitude than that of the Euphrates, so in ancient times irrigation canals were dug from the Euphrates to the Tigris, the latter receiving the tailings of canals between the rivers. Apparently the Tigris did not carry as much silt as the Euphrates.

The Tigris was the great river of Assyria; on the banks stood most of the important Assyrian cities: those mentioned in the Bible include Nineveh, Calah, and Ashur.

The Euphrates

The Euphrates is mentioned in Genesis 2:14 as one of the rivers of Eden and appears frequently in the Old Testament (in eight books) and in Revelation (9:14; 16:12) because it is the river of Mesopotamia closer to Palestine and Syria. It rises on the northern slopes of the Taurus Mountains and winds its way over a meandering 1700-mile path to the Persian Gulf. As it flows from the mountains, it first goes in a southwesterly course toward the Mediterranean, coming to within 90 miles of that sea; then it bends sharply toward the southeast. In Syria it has two tributaries from the east or north: the Balikh and Khabur. Like the Tigris, its lower course has changed considerably during historical times: the ancient channel flowed past Kish and Nippur in the south. As its bed has moved westward, the river has been less useful to man. Since a majority of irrigation canals led from the east bank to the Tigris, the increasing distance put a heavy strain on the labor force of the area.

Also, like the Tigris, the Euphrates floods annually. The waters begin to rise about the middle of March, continue to rise until June, and recede to ordinary levels in September. The flooding of the rivers of Mesopotamia did not prove to be the blessing to the area that the flooding of the Nile was in Egypt. The flood came while crops were growing, and dikes were required to protect the land. Late flooding increased salinization of the soil (see discussion below) because of rapid evaporation in increasingly high temperatures. Mud suspended in the swollen rivers was less fertile than that carried by the Nile and could not be immediately deposited on fields, so it clogged the irrigation canals that carried the water inland and required that canals be redredged or replaced by new ones.

In the neighborhood of Hit in the middle Euphrates northwest of Baghdad are extensive bitumen lakes, which supplied the ancients with material for cementing bricks and caulking boats. From Hit to where the Tigris and Euphrates join lies broad, flat alluvium. At Hit the river is 250 yards across and from this point on decreases in size because there are no tributaries and its water is used for irrigation. The current of the Euphrates is 5 miles per hour at high water and 1½ miles per hour at low water. Much of the river is interrupted by rapids, and navigation is difficult except at high water.

Most of the great biblical cities of Babylonia—Babylon, Ur, Erech, and many others—were located along the Euphrates. This was true, of course, because the river was necessary for irrigation—for the sustaining of life. Not only did the river make possible the development of cities, it required urbanization. The reason for this is easy to understand. Because the river came to flood stage while crops stood in the fields, it was necessary to build dikes along the banks. And since the river carried so much silt in its waters, it tended to raise the level of its bed, forcing the dikes ever higher. Thus, during part of its course, the river bed stood at some height above the surrounding land. Tapping of the river for irrigation purposes therefore required large irrigation canals with dikes of their own and a vast system of subsidiary canals. Only in this way could the tremendous pressure of flood waters be handled. The development and maintenance of this system required a massive amount of organized labor. Individual farmers could not do the job. So as peoples of the Mesopotamian plain sought to harness the river for their sustenance, they had to collect themselves together into city-states to get the job done.

Mesopotamian Prosperity

As they did so, they became prosperous and built an advanced civilization. Their success stirred envy in the hearts of the mountain peoples along the eastern fringes of Mesopotamia and the desert peoples of the Arabian peninsula to the west and south. Envy and at times dire necessity led to periodic invasion, against which there were no natural barriers. These infusions of new ethnic stock and new cultural elements created in the Mesopotamian valley a heterogeneous culture. In the Nile Valley, on the other hand, barriers to invasion permitted the maintenance of a relatively homogeneous culture.

The degree of wealth and cultural sophistication of ancient Mesopotamia becomes quite surprising when one considers the lack of natural resources of the area. Ancient Mesopotamians were singularly a "have-not" people. Since the soil of much of the region was alluvial, it had no mineral deposits, no stone or great timber resources. The people had little more than sun and soil and water to work with. In a very real sense they became people of the soil. On the soil they grew their foodstuffs (dates, wheat, emmer, millet, sesame, and especially barley were among key items) and their clothing (wool from sheep and linen from flax). From the clay they made pottery in which to store and prepare their food and from which to eat it. From the clay they also made bricks (baked and unbaked) for construction of houses and public buildings, and tablets on which to keep their records and do their assignments in school. Reeds caulked with bitumen and inflated animal skins provided materials for boats and rafts and thus a means of traveling on the rivers. Agricultural surplus could be traded abroad for metals, timber, and other necessities and luxuries.

Climate

The importance of the Tigris and Euphrates to the maintenance of life in Mesopotamia is clear when one looks at the climate and rainfall pattern of the area. In Baghdad, temperatures hit 120°-140° F. in the sun and about 108° F. in the shade during July and August. Even higher temperatures occur in southern Iraq near the Persian Gulf. Some regions there, baked under cloudless skies, are among the hottest places on earth. At least in most of the southern part of Mesopotamia there is rarely ever rain in the summer. Even in the rainy season there is commonly not more than 6 or 7 inches. And, unfortunately, this meager amount is not constant, for Baghdad has been known to receive as much as 22 inches or as little as 2 inches per year. In the hill country, the annual average is about 16 inches; the mountains receive double that amount. Under such conditions, the waters of the Tigris and Euphrates are a necessity for the maintenance of life. Unfortunately, however, the rivers do not prove to be an unmixed blessing. Low waters mean drought and famine. Excessive flooding brings catastrophe when rivers break through their embankments, submerge land, and sweep away the mud houses. Although flood control projects make this a less likely threat today, ancient Mesopotamia hovered between a state of swamp and desert.

Geographical Divisions

As has been indicated, there are regional differences in Mesopotamia. The southern part, from the area around Baghdad (where the rivers come closest together) to the Persian Gulf, is flat, alluvial soil and is commonly called Babylonia. What the earliest peoples called it is not known, but by 2000 B.C. inhabitants were calling it Sumer and Akkad, after the Sumerians and Akkadians who lived there. Sumer was the region just north of the Persian Gulf and Akkad the area around ancient Babylon or modern Baghdad. Southern Mesopotamia was also called Chaldea after the Chaldeans came into it about 1000 B.C. In several passages the Old Testament speaks of Shinar, which clearly applies to Babylonia, though efforts to equate Shinar and Sumer linguistically now have been abandoned.

Assyria occupied northern Mesopotamia and was composed of land that was sometimes hilly and even mountainous in the north. So Assyria had greater supplies of stone and some timber in the early days. She had districts that enjoyed enough rainfall to practice dry farming. It was therefore not so necessary to band together in the north to maintain the agricultural system as it was in the south, and Assyria had a larger class of yeoman farmers. The boundaries of Assyria were more fluid than those of Babylonia, depending on the relative strength of peoples living in Syria and Asia Minor.

Coastline of the Persian Gulf

That the Tigris and Euphrates have carried billions of tons of soil southward in their muddy waters and deposited it somewhere is certain. The old standard view subscribed to in most textbooks is that the rivers dropped this soil at their mouths and pushed the coastline of the Persian Gulf ever southward. In fact, the entire area below Babylon is supposed to have been formed in that way. Presumably, the Tigris and Euphrates did not join in earlier days, but flowed as separate streams into the gulf.

On the basis of newer studies in geology, however, that view is being seriously questioned. It is argued that, although the rivers bring down much silt, some 90 percent apparently is deposited before reaching the gulf. Tremendous deposits, up to more than 30 feet in depth, have been laid in southern Mesopotamia. But the rise of the land level has not been marked in this area. So the theory has been advanced that the Tigris and Euphrates drop their sediment in a slowly subsiding basin. Without question, the subterranean water level has risen over the centuries, because, for example, the Babylon of Hammurabi (about 1700 B.C.) is now under water and cannot be excavated. The gradual sinking of the land level supposedly has prevented the land elevation or the coastline from changing significantly since Old Testament times, and the two Mesopotamian rivers are believed always to have flowed into the gulf as a single stream.

While many geologists have followed the new theories, archaeologists have not been so quick to do so. Excavations and textual information indicate that Ur and Eridu, for instance, had easy access to the sea in Old Testament times. Ur had a seaport, and, at the minimum, the 150 miles of waterway between Ur and the gulf must have been more open than at present. Moreover, recent geological investigations in southern Iraq indicate that even into historic times the shore of the gulf may have run anywhere from 80 to 175 miles northwest of its present line.[1] Further study of textual, archaeological, geological, and hydrographical data is necessary in order to solve this knotty problem.

---

1. Leonard Woolley, *Ur of the Chaldees*, ed. P. R. S. Moorey, rev. ed. (London: Herbert, 1982), p. 20. See also Moorey's bibliographical notes on p. 35.

The Decline of Mesopotamia

In biblical times, Mesopotamia was fertile and prosperous. Today one can look for miles across the flat plains and see nothing but brown and barren land. What has happened? For one thing, the Euphrates River has shifted its course westward, leaving numerous southern Mesopotamian cities without the life-giving waters necessary for their existence and making the whole irrigation system more difficult to maintain. Second, the ancient empires that gave so much attention to maintaining the irrigation system passed off the scene, and the system fell into decay. Third, Tamerlane's destructiveness at the end of the fourteenth century was of a magnitude and cruelty that is hard to imagine. Dikes and canals wrecked at that time were never restored under the long Turkish occupation, and the region has fallen into utter ruin. But the real enemy of prosperity in this region is salinization of the soil.

Today one can see in many places a coat of salt on the surface of the soil. Even in other areas where no such extreme situation exists, crops cannot be grown. Barley, with a high salt toleration, will not bear fruit if there is more than one percent of salt in the soil. The date palm will not yield fruit if salt content is more than two percent. Because of salinization of the soil, population began to drift out of southern Mesopotamia to the northern regions in the third century B.C. Salinization comes from two sources: irrigation and the water table. Irrigation waters were slightly saline (containing a combination of calcium, magnesium, and sodium); and when they stood on the land and evaporated there under the hot sun of the area, the cumulative effect of the deposit they left could be damaging. Extensive rains that might wash salts from the soil did not exist. In some places saline groundwater rose to the roots of growing crops; this often occurred because new waters, added as a result of excessive irrigation, rains, or floods, can raise the level of the water table considerably when drainage systems are poor. Although the salinization problems is acute in large areas of southern Mesopotamia today, making it virtually impossible to restore former productivity, the situation is not so severe in the north, where the water table does not rise dangerously close to the roots of growing crops.

PALESTINE

SCALE OF MILES
0 5 10 20 30 40 50

MEDITERRANEAN SEA
THE GREAT SEA

SIDON
PHOENICIA
DAMASCUS
▲ MT. HERMON
LEBANON MOUNTAINS

TYRE
DAN

ROSH HA-NIQRA
HAZOR
Lake Huleh
BASHAN
PLAIN OF ACRE
GALILEE
CHORAZIN
ACCHO
CAPERNAUM
SEA OF GALILEE
TIBERIAS
NAZARETH
Brook Kishon
Yarmuk River
MT. CARMEL
PLAIN OF ESDRAELON
▲ MT. TABOR
MEGIDDO

CAESAREA
▲ MT. GILBOA
Jordan River
GILEAD

PLAIN OF SHARON
SAMARIA
• SAMARIA
Jabbok River
SHECHEM • ▲ MT. EBAL
▲ MT. GERIZIM
Yarkon River
EPHRAIM

JOPPA
PLAIN OF PHILISTIA
BETHEL
EKRON
JERICHO
AMMON
▲ MT. NEBO
VALLEY OF ELAH
JERUSALEM
ASHKELON
ASHDOD
BETHLEHEM
PLAIN
GATH
• LACHISH
SHEPHELAH
DEAD (SALT) SEA
GAZA
HEBRON
Arnon River

JUDEA
MOAB
• BEERSHEBA

WADI EL-ARISH
Zered River

NEGEV

EDOM

• PETRA

2

Palestine

Palestine is preeminently the land of the Bible. Here Abraham, Isaac, and Jacob lived for 215 years during the patriarchal period before the entire clan of the Hebrews moved to Egypt. Most of the book of Genesis is occupied with this narrative. Here Abraham's descendants returned to live during the days of the conquest; the judges; the united kingdom under Saul, David, and Solomon; and the divided kingdoms of Israel and Judah. The account of these events appears in Joshua, Judges, 1 and 2 Samuel, 1 and 2 Kings, and 1 and 2 Chronicles. Although many Hebrews were deported by Assyria and Babylonia, some continued to live in the land during the captivity. Hebrews were in the land in force once more in the days of restoration under Persian auspices (see Ezra, Nehemiah, Esther). And the gospels and Acts record that this is the land where the Lord Jesus and the early disciples lived and worked. Although it may not be possible to walk in their footsteps today, one may visit some of the sites they knew.

The land has been called by various names, according to the people who occupied it. The older name of the land, Canaan, appears in Scripture as early as Genesis 11:31. Sometimes it has been known as the land of the Amorites or the land of Israel; but, for the last couple of millennia, it has commonly been known as Palestine. This name is derived from the Philistines, who settled on the coastal plain. Their land, Philistia, was called by the Greeks *Palaistine* and by the Romans *Palaestina*, hence the English name *Palestine*.

Palestine is a land bridge between the two oldest civilizations in the world—Mesopotamia and Egypt. But its civilization was immensely different from both of them. They were made possible by irrigation of river systems. Palestine, on the other hand, could engage in dry farming because there was adequate rainfall in much of the area. Rainfall varies, however: 25 inches in Nazareth in Galilee, 16 inches at Tiberias on the Sea of Galilee, 22 inches in the Valley of Jezreel, 32-36 inches on Mount Carmel, 22 inches at Jerusalem, 8 inches at Beersheba, and 6 inches at Jericho.[1] The scenery of Mesopotamia and Egypt is monotonous; in Palestine there is variety. In fact, it is probably true that no other country in the world offers such a variety of scenery and climate in such a small area. As a land bridge, Palestine has been so frequently invaded and so often dominated by foreign powers that it could not develop the high degree of cultural homogeneity found in Egypt or the lesser degree in Mesopotamia.

Borders

It is difficult to be specific about the borders of Palestine. From the Old Testament perspective, one would judge that the boundaries of Canaan were the Jordan River and the Mediterranean on the east and west, and Dan and Beersheba on the north and south (Judges 20:1; 1 Samuel 3:20). The distance from Dan to Beersheba is just under 150 miles. The width of the country at the Sea of Galilee is 25-30 miles; at the northern end of the Dead Sea, about 55 miles; and at the southern end of the Dead Sea, about 85 miles. This area totals some 6,000 to 7,000 square miles and would be about the size of Connecticut and Delaware combined. It seems, however, that the Hebrews sometimes controlled additional territory west of the Jordan, as well as the highlands east of the Jordan (about 4,000 square miles). At the outside, then, they normally controlled no more than 10,000 to 12,000 square miles—about the size of Maryland or a little less than that of Belgium.

───────────

1. As a supplement to the rain, dew falls in the coastal plain about 250 nights of the year and in the hills between 100 and 180 nights per year. It varies, as does the rainfall. The dew is, of course, very beneficial to summer vegetation. God observed that the Hebrews would have this agricultural benefit, even before they conquered Palestine (Deuteronomy 33:28).

Of course, the Hebrew Empire at its height under David and Solomon was larger than that.

One should not confuse the land of Canaan with the promised land. The latter as spelled out to Abraham extended "from the river of Egypt unto . . . the river Euphrates" (Genesis 15:18). The Hebrew word translated "river" in Genesis 15:18 refers to an ever-flowing river and apparently must be applied to the Nile; other streams of southern Palestine and the Sinai flow only during the rainy season. The eastern-most branch of the Nile, the Pelusiac, flows out near modern Port Said and hence near the ancient line of fortifications which protected Egypt from marauding Asiatics. Thus, the Pelusiac branch could properly be thought of as the border of Egypt. The distance from Port Said to the Euphrates may be variously measured—in a straight line or in an arc. The former would be some 650 to 700 miles. Of course the Jews have never enjoyed possession of all this land; fulfillment of the prophecy must be reserved for the millennial day at the end times.

Climate

Palestine enjoys a moderate climate. January is the coldest month with average temperatures as follows: 46°-50° F. at Jerusalem, 53° in the coastal plain, and 53°-55° in the Jordan Valley. August is the warmest month and has mean temperatures of 71°-79° F. at Jerusalem, 75°-79° in the coastal plain, and 82°-93° in the Jordan Valley. The highest known temperature to date in the Jordan Valley was registered at 129° F. in June 1941; at that same time the highest known temperature in Jerusalem stood at 111°. The lowest known temperature at Jerusalem was 24° F. and in Lower Galilee was 8.6° (both in February 1950).

Divisions of the Land

As noted above, Palestine has a varied topography and climate. The land divides into five longitudinal divisions and two lateral regions. Along the Mediterranean extends the coastal plain, east of which rises the foothills or piedmont or Shephelah. Farther east stands the Western Plateau or Western Mountain Ridge or Central Mountain Ridge. Then comes the Great Rift of the Jordan Valley, east of which rises the

5 Eastern Plateau or Eastern Mountain Ridge. The 'northern lateral region is the Plain of Esdraelon, which extends from Mount Carmel to the Jordan Valley. And the ²southern lateral zone, which cuts across the southern Palestine from the Mediterranean to the south end of the Dead Sea, is the Negev.

The Coastal Plain

The coastal plain extends from the Wadi el-Arish to Rosh ha-Niqra or the Ladder of Tyre at the present Lebanese-Israeli border—a distance of some 150 miles. In the north it is less than 3 miles wide, but it gradually increases to about 25 miles near Gaza. The altitude gently rises from sea level to about 500 feet. Along most of the coast, which is very straight and poor in promontories and bays, is a belt of arid sand dunes. These block the outflow of the small rivers and create marshes. The coastline itself may consist of either a gently inclined shore with a beach or precipitous cliffs 30 to 120 feet in height. The nature of the coastline tended to force the building of towns of any size and importance a short distance inland. The same was true of the main coastal road. Both because of occupational preferences of the Hebrews (farmers, herders, vine dressers, etc.) and the lack of good harbors, the Hebrews did not build any Mediterranean ports worthy of the name in Old Testament times. Not until just before the birth of Christ did Herod the Great construct the magnificent port at Caesarea (about 25 miles south of Haifa), naming it after Augustus Caesar. The city was a typical Greco-Roman center with its hippodrome (seating 20,000), amphitheater, theater, aqueducts, temples, and colonnaded street. The port was protected by a massive breakwater. Caesarea was the capital of Palestine during Paul's ministry, and there he was imprisoned for two years (Acts 23-27). There too began the bloody struggle that ended with the destruction of Jerusalem and the Temple in A.D. 70.

The coastal plain subdivides into three regions. On the north lies the Plain of Acre (Accho), which is about 20 miles long between Rosh ha-Niqra and Mount Carmel. Its width increases from around 3 miles in the north to 10 miles in the south. Acre is the main town of the plain, and a river that flows through the plain into Haifa Bay is the Kishon—of some interest because Elijah slew the prophets of Baal by its banks (1 Kings 18:40).

The central part of the coastal plain is called Sharon and extends about 50 miles from Mount Carmel to the Yarkon River near Tel Aviv-Joppa, though the southern boundary of the plain is not clearly distinguished. It varies from 6 to 12 miles in breadth. Joppa, at its southern end, served as the main port of Jerusalem, even though it was poorly protected from the sea. In ancient times Sharon was heavily forested and had luxuriant vegetation and extensive pasture lands (see, e.g., 1 Chronicles 5:16; 27:29).

The Plain of Philistia in the south is about 70 miles long and reaches a width of 25 miles opposite Beersheba. Although rainfall decreases in the south, there is enough moisture for growing crops as far south as Gaza. Gaza was the most southerly and the main city of the plain. Farther north stood Ashkelon and Ashdod. These three joined with Gath and Ekron in the Shephelah to form the Philistine pentapolis. This combination of power posed a threat to the freedom and independence of the Hebrews for two centuries.

The Shephelah

The Shephelah[2], or piedmont, or foothills, rise east of the coastal plain to an average altitude of 500 to 1000 feet, though some points are as much as 1500 feet high. It is a well-defined transitional section about 40 miles long from north to south and 8 miles east and west. Apparently plentiful forests blanketed the hills of the Shephelah in Old Testament times (1 Kings 10:27). Three important valleys cross this hilly region. At its northern limits is the Valley of Ajalon (Aijalon), beginning 5 miles northwest of Jerusalem, where Joshua decisively defeated the Canaanites (Joshua 10:12). It is the gate to Jerusalem from the Plain of Sharon. Some 10 miles to the south and immediately west of Jerusalem is the Valley of Sorek, scene of numerous exploits of Samson (e.g., Judges 16:4). Another 7 to 8 miles farther south is the Valley of Elah, where David killed Goliath (1 Samuel 17:2). Since these valleys led into the heart of Judah, it is understandable that their control would be disputed between Philistines and Hebrews.

---

2. This Hebrew term, meaning "to be low," is variously translated in the Old Testament: "vale" (Deuteronomy 1:7; Joshua 10:40); "valley" (Joshua 11:2); "low plains" (1 Chronicles 27:28). See also Joshua 9:1; 11:16 twice; 12:8; 15:33; Judges 1:9; 1 Kings 10:27; 2 Chronicles 1:15; 9:27; 26:10; 28:18; Jeremiah 17:26; 32:44; 33:13; Obadiah 19; Zechariah 7:7.

The Western Plateau

Interests of many Bible students center on the Western Plateau or the Western Mountain Ridge sector of Palestine. Among these hills and valleys of Galilee, Samaria, and Judea took place a great many Old and New Testament events. Here lived a wide variety of individuals, from faithful Abraham to faithless Judas, from saintly Hezekiah to reprobate Ahab, from devout Hannah to scheming Jezebel. And, of course, special significance attaches to Christ's earthly ministry in all three parts of this region.

Although many for convenience look at the western ridge as something of a unit, each of the three parts has its own characteristics. Judea has more compact hills, while in Samaria they are more scattered, and in Galilee the low hills of the south gradually ascend as one goes northward. A rough approximation is that the altitude of the whole ridge ranges from 2,000 to 4,000 feet.

Galilee. The hill regions of Galilee are clearly defined. On the west they touch the coastal plain, in the north they stop at the gorge of the Litani River, in the east they border on the Jordan Valley, and in the south they rise above the Valley of Jezreel. It is customary to make a distinction between Lower and Upper Galilee. The hills of southern or Lower Galilee reach a maximum of 2,000 feet. Mount Gilboa (1,640 ft.) stands at the south of Lower Galilee while Mount Tabor (1,929 ft.) rises in the north. Upper Galilee has heights ranging from 2,000 to 4,000 feet. Between the two parts of Galilee the fault of Esh-Shaghur cuts across the country at about the latitude of the north end of the Sea of Galilee. Galilee has adequate rainfall and fertile soil and thus has attractive agricultural and pastoral possibilities. In ancient times it had a considerable forest cover. Its numerous roads leading to all parts of Canaan and adjacent lands contributed to a greater cosmopolitanism than was true of other parts of Palestine.

Samaria. Samaria is separated from Galilee by the Valley of Jezreel on the north and from Judah on the south by a less pronounced division along the line of the Valley of the Craftsmen (Nehemiah 11:35) and the Valley of Ajalon to Bethel and thence by other valleys to Jericho. On the east is the Jordan Valley; and on the west, the Plain of Sharon. As already noted, in the region of Samaria the hills are not closely compacted together, leaving stretches of good land with abundant rainfall for growing crops and foothills for grazing purposes. Olive and grape production was extensive here, as was the raising of barley and wheat. It is to be remembered that Jesus was in Samaria when He uttered His famous observation about the fields being already white and ready for harvest (John 4:35), signifying the urgency of preaching the gospel. The hills of the entire area were apparently heavily wooded in biblical times. The tribes of Ephraim and half of Manasseh occupied the highlands of Samaria, and these descendants of Joseph buried their progenitor near Shechem; there one may see Joseph's traditional tomb today.

Several places in Samaria have biblical significance. The permanent capital of the Northern Kingdom (kingdom of Israel) was located on the hill of Samaria 35 miles north of Jerusalem. Here Omri and Ahab built their palaces. The hill rises to a height of 300 feet above a fruitful valley, and ravines on all sides contributed to its defensive capability. Herod the Great rebuilt the site and gave it the character of a typical Greco-Roman city with a hippodrome, theater, and temple to Augustus. Previously, the capital of the Northern Kingdom had been at Shechem (about 7 miles southeast of Samaria) and at Tirzah. At Shechem the patriarchs stayed (Genesis 12:6; 35:4), Joshua delivered his farewell address (Joshua 24:1), and later the kingdom was divided (1 Kings 12:1). Shechem stood in a valley between the famous mountains Ebal (on the north, 3,100 feet high) and Gerizim (on the south, 2,900 feet high). On the former, six tribes stood to hear the curses for disobedience to the law; and on the latter, six tribes stood to bless the people for obedience (Deuteronomy 27-28).

Judea. The highlands of Judea extend about 60 miles from Bethel to Beersheba and have an average elevation range of 2,000 to 3,000 feet. On the west they are bounded by the Shephelah; and on the east by the Jordan Valley. Access from the latter into the Judean highlands is difficult. A good north-south road ran near the eastern edge of the highlands, and along it stood such important cities as Jerusalem, Bethlehem, and Hebron. Judea has good soil, especially good for fruit trees and vines; but it must be retained by terraces on the hillsides. Just west of Jerusalem is the watershed, beyond which begins the Judean Desert. East of the watershed line, Judea is almost completely desert; what rainfall there is descends the steep slopes rapidly and cuts deep wadis (stream beds that are dry during the summer). Although rainfall in the highest hills of Judea may be as much as 28 inches a year, about 6 miles east of Jerusalem it dwindles to 12 inches and around the Dead Sea to 2 to 4 inches. The wilderness of Judea on various occasions in history has given refuge to separatists from society, whether by choice (as in the case of the Qumran community) or pursuit (as in the case of David—Ziph is about 3 miles southeast of Hebron).

Jerusalem is, of course, the most famous of all Judean cities and assumed importance for the Hebrews after David captured it and made it his capital. At that time the fortified area was located on the hill Ophel and covered about eleven acres, as recent excavations have shown.[3] It stood where the valleys of the Kidron, Hinnom, and Tyropoeon come together. Actually, however, Jerusalem came to occupy five hills in ancient times (Ophel, Moriah, Bezetha, Acra, Zion), the highest of which is about 2,550 feet above sea level. To the east of the Kidron Valley stands the Mount of Olives (2,680 feet above sea level), part of a ridge that divides Jerusalem from the wilderness of Judea.

Bethlehem, 6 miles to the south of Jerusalem, is slightly higher in altitude; and Hebron, 23 miles south of Jerusalem, is 3,300 feet in altitude, the highest town in Judah. Although Hebron was important for its connection with numerous events in Scripture, it is especially known for the Cave of Machpelah, where Abraham and various other members of the patriarchal family were buried. Today the cave is generally considered to be under the city mosque at Hebron. At the southern edge of Judea, about 50 miles from Jerusalem, stands Beersheba at an altitude of 1,000 feet. Jerusalem, Hebron, and Beersheba all gain significance from the fact that they are at crossroads, located on important routes north and south and east and west.

The Jordan Rift

The fourth longitudinal division of Palestine is the Jordan Rift, which extends some 300 miles from Mount Hermon to the Red Sea.[4] This deep depression has an average width of 10 miles and descends to a depth of about 1,300 feet at the shore of the Dead Sea, the lowest spot

---

3. Kathleen Kenyon, *Royal Cities of the Old Testament* (New York: Schocken, 1971), p. 32.
4. Actually, this rift is part of a geological fault that extends more than 4,000 miles from northern Syria through the Red Sea and down into the great lakes of East Africa.

on earth. More important, however, is the fact that the mountains generally rise steeply and abruptly to a height of 3,000 feet and more above the valley floor. There are few places where the topography moderates and the Jordan may be crossed easily. Thus the rift is an effective dividing line between Palestine west of Jordan and Transjordan. It does not matter, then, that the Jordan River itself is not especially wide or deep, for the real barrier is not the river but the rift.

Towering over the northern end of the Jordan Valley is Mount Hermon, 9,232 feet above sea level. From the slopes of Hermon comes most of the water for the Jordan,[5] which has four sources. The Hasbani flows from the western slope of Hermon, and the Baniyas (Banyasi) from the southwestern slope of Hermon; the Liddani (Leddan) originates at Dan, and from the northwest comes the Bareighit. These four join about 5 miles south of Dan and flow as a single stream another 10 miles into Lake Huleh at 220 feet above sea level. The Huleh region used to be a swampy area surrounding a lake about 4 by 3 miles in extent. Israeli engineers have drained the area and reclaimed 15,000 acres of excellent farmland and improved the condition of another 15,000 acres that was often too muddy when rains were heavy.

Dominating the Huleh valley at the southwest was Hazor, standing at the junction of the north-south road and the route to Damascus—which crossed the Jordan just below the lake. Hazor consisted of two parts: a 25-acre mound and a rectangular 175-acre enclosure to the north, some 1,000 yards long by 700 yards wide. This was the largest city of Palestine in Canaanite times, with a population of 40,000.[6] Joshua defeated Jabin I of Hazor, who headed a northern confederacy at the time of the conquest (Joshua 11:10-14). Later, a second Jabin of Hazor met defeat at the hands of judges Deborah and Barak (Judges 4).

Some 10 miles south of Huleh the Jordan flows into the Sea of Galilee. This pear-shaped lake (Sea of Galilee, Lake Kinneret, Sea of Chinnereth, Lake of Gennesaret or Sea of Tiberias) is 13 miles long and 7 miles wide at its greatest extent and covers 64 square miles. Its surface varies between 684 and 710 feet below sea level, depending on amounts of rainfall; and its deepest part is 833 feet below the Mediter-

5. Mount Hermon has an average annual rainfall of 60 inches.
6. Yigael Yadin, "Excavations at Hazor," *The Biblical Archaeologist*, February 1956, p. 11.

ranean or about 150 feet below the surface of the lake. At its northwest lies the plain of Gennesaret and around the northern and western sides stood Chorazin, Capernaum, and Tiberias. Bethsaida was almost certainly on its northeastern shore. The idyllic beauty and quiet of the Sea of Galilee today do not even hint at conditions during New Testament times. Then bustling towns stood at or near the shore. Fishing boats dotted the surface, and grain boats often crossed over from the east.

As the Jordan continues its southerly course, it descends until at the surface of the Dead Sea it drops to 1,308 feet below sea level.[7] The distance between the Sea of Galilee and the Dead Sea is about 65 miles in a straight line, but the river often flows as the snake slithers and has a bed of some 200 miles. The Jordan's average width is 90 to 100 feet during most of the year but is considerably wider at flood stage. Important tributaries flow into the Jordan south of the Sea of Galilee; chief of these are the Yarmuk and the Jabbok, both of which flow down from the eastern highlands. In the region where the Jabbok flows into the Jordan and for some distance southward stands the Zor. This is an impenetrable jungle about a mile wide that still harbors wild beasts, though the lion is no longer numbered among them.

The Dead Sea is 50 miles long and 11 miles wide, and in its northern basin it is 1,300 feet deep in spots. Its southern basin averages only about 20 feet in depth (maximum of 30-35 ft.),[8] however, and is commonly thought to cover Sodom and the other cities of the plain. Since the Dead Sea has no outlet and is subject to high evaporation by the heat of the area (plus inflow of water from mineral springs), its saline content regularly increases. It is now over 30 percent salts in solution at the surface of the southern basin and 33 percent at depth, the highest salt content of any lake in the world and several times that of the great oceans or seas. Numerous chemicals exist in the Dead Sea, and some are now being extracted by Israeli firms. About 7 miles northwest of the Dead Sea stood Old Testament Jericho, gateway to central Palestine. A mile or two from Old Testament Jericho the Herodian family later built up New Testament Jericho.

South of the Dead Sea is the Arabah, 115 miles in length. This narrow valley rises at its floor to about 725 feet above sea level. Though a desert region, it was valuable for its copper resources; and at

---

7. This figure varies from year to year, depending on amounts of rainfall.
8. See note 7 above.

its southern end Solomon built an important seaport near where modern Israelis maintain the port of Eilat.

Transjordan

Transjordan includes the area between the Jordan Rift and the
Syrian Desert. This consists of Bashan in the north, from Mount
Hermon and the Hauran Mountains to the Yarmuk (35 miles); Gilead,
between the Yarmuk and Jabbok Rivers (35 miles); Ammon and
Moab, between the Jabbok and Zered Rivers (80 miles); and Edom,
from the Zered to the Gulf of Aqabah (100 miles).

Bashan. Bashan has more rainfall than the rest of Transjordan, and
its 70-mile-wide belt of fertile basalt soil made it the granary of the
Levant in ancient times. Its elevation ranges from 700 to 1,600 feet in
the plateau region. At the northern rim of the plateau, peaks rise to
more than 4,000 feet and one reaches 5,900 feet. In Jesus' day this was
the Tetrarchy of Philip and included Ituraea, Gaulanitis, Auranitis, and
Batanaea.

Gilead. Gilead is similar to the Western Mountain Ridge with an
altitude of 2,000 to 4,000 feet. It has a plateau in the north and a
mountainous region in the south where rainfall approximates 30 inches
per year. The region of settlement is 30 to 40 miles wide.

Moab and Ammon. The Moab plateau is about 20 to 30 miles wide
opposite the Dead Sea and has an altitude of about 4,000 feet. Its rainfall
is reasonably reliable and adequate for grain production, as the book of
Ruth attests. Mount Nebo, a promontory from which Moses saw the
Promised Land, juts westward from the Moab plateau and reaches an
altitude of 2,630 feet. Thus, it towers over the Dead Sea and the Jordan
Valley. In New Testament times, Gilead and the northern part of
Ammon were known as Perea, part of the kingdom of Herod Antipas.

Edom. Edom is more mountainous than Gilead, Moab, and Bashan
to the north, with heights often exceeding 5,000 feet. The southern
part of the area gets very little rainfall, but in the north the annual
average is 16 to 20 inches. During the period of the Hebrew monarchy,
the capital was Sela ("rock"), built on a flat-topped crag at the southern
end of the mountain-ringed valley. Sela became Petra. The kingdom
derived its economic strength from agriculture, mineral resources, and
tolls levied on caravans crossing its territory. In the third century B.C.,

the Nabateans occupied Edom and drove the Edomites into southern Judah. The family of Herod the Great was of Idumean (Edomite) stock. Apparently Petra enjoyed its most prosperous period under Nabatean control.

The Lateral Regions

Esdraelon. The northern lateral region of Palestine is the Plain of Esdraelon, which extends northwest and southeast and is about 24 miles in length from Mount Carmel to Mount Gilboa. The region varies in altitude from 60 to 160 feet, and the soil is dark, heavy, and rich in organic matter. Its fertility compares favorably with that of the Nile delta. Esdraelon lies astride all important lines of communication in northern Palestine and was the scene of many struggles reported in and outside of Scripture. Dominating the southern flank of the valley is the mound of Megiddo, which was one of the most important towns of ancient Palestinian history. Solomon fortified it to help maintain his empire, and Ahab improved on Solomon's earlier efforts. In the last times the great War of Armageddon will center on the valley (also called Valley of Jezreel and Armageddon).[9] Mount Carmel overshadows Esdraelon on the west. Twenty miles long at its base, Carmel reaches 9 miles at its greatest width. Its greatest height is 1,792 feet, but the traditional site of the struggle between Elijah and the prophets of Baal is at Qeren ha-Karmel at 1,581 feet in altitude.

The Negev. The great southern lateral region of Palestine is the Negev. It is roughly a triangle, with its base at the southern edge of the Judean hills and its apex on the Gulf of Aqaba. At its base it is about 70 miles wide, and the total area is about 4,600 square miles, the size of Connecticut. The altitude of the Eilat hills in the south reaches 3,000 feet. The central Negev hills, which occupy more than half of the region, are slightly higher. In the Beersheba region, altitude ranges from about 150 feet to 1,650 feet and is 800 feet at Beersheba itself. Rainfall in the north is about 14 inches per year and is considerably less in the south. Although it is debated whether there has been a great

---

9. Esdraelon may refer to the western part of this plain and Jezreel its eastern part. The western part is also called the Valley of Har Megiddo (or "mound of Megiddo"), or Armageddon. Unfortunately, Bible commentators and even the basic reference works do not standardly distinguish the use of those terms.

change in the climate of the Negev since biblical times, it is certain that ancients knew better than more recent inhabitants how to utilize water resources. In Abraham's day and subsequently, there was a considerable number of settlements in this now virtually desert and uninhabited region. Although important trade and communication lines crossed the Negev, not the least of which was Solomon's route to his port at Ezion-geber, the region was an important buffer against Israel's enemies, who would find it hard to attack across such an inhospitable region. Israeli engineers have piped water from the Galilee region into the Negev, and numerous settlers are once again causing the desert to blossom as a rose.

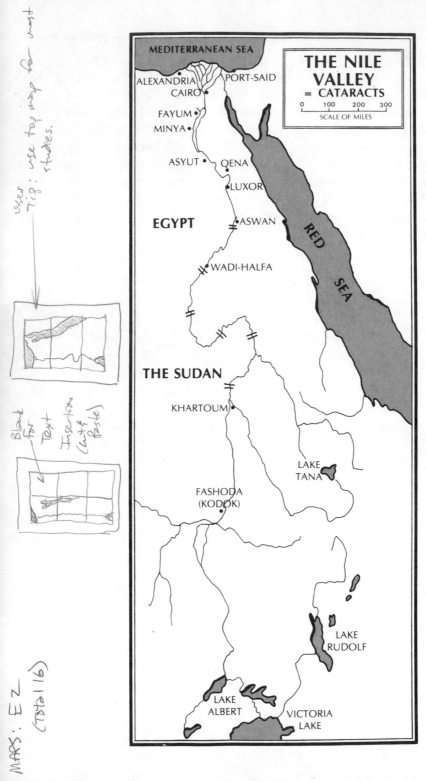

MEDITERRANEAN SEA

ALEXANDRIA
CAIRO
PORT-SAID

**THE NILE
VALLEY**
= CATARACTS

0   100   200   300
SCALE OF MILES

FAYUM
MINYA

ASYUT
QENA
LUXOR

EGYPT

ASWAN

WADI-HALFA

RED
SEA

THE SUDAN

KHARTOUM

LAKE
TANA

FASHODA
(KODOK)

LAKE
RUDOLF

LAKE
ALBERT
VICTORIA
LAKE

3

Egypt

Egypt is commonly thought of as the land of the pyramids, the pharaohs, and the Nile. Its glorious past stirs historical and cultural interest and sometimes even religious interests when students investigate the host of fearsome animal-headed gods the ancients worshiped there.

But Egypt is also a Bible land. Early in the history of mankind, soon after the Flood, descendants of Noah went down into Egypt. Genesis 10:6 mentions a son of Ham (Noah's son), Mizraim, who was progenitor of a large clan of people. *Mizraim* is the Hebrew word for Egypt and must here indicate that this descendant of Noah was father of the Egyptian people. Many centuries later, Egypt figures in the biblical narrative again in connection with the life of Abraham. After the patriarch left Mesopotamia and settled in Palestine, a famine struck the area where he was living; so he went into Egypt to obtain food and to live until the famine was over (Genesis 12:10-20). Subsequently Sarah, Abraham's wife, when she proved incapable of bearing children, gave him an Egyptian servant girl to wife. From this union was born Ishmael, progenitor of the Arabs (Genesis 16).

Later on, God gave Abraham a son by Sarah—Isaac, who in turn had a son named Jacob, or Israel. Israel fathered sons who were ancestors of the twelve tribes of Israel. In Jacob's old age, at the invitation of Joseph and the reigning pharaoh, he took all his large family into Egypt to escape famine, as his grandfather Abraham had done (Genesis 46). This time the Hebrews remained in Egypt for 430 years (Exodus 12:40-41). The last fourteen chapters of Genesis and the first fourteen chapters of Exodus take their setting in Egypt. At first the Hebrews enjoyed good treatment at the hands of the Egyptians, but they were later reduced to slavery and eventually escaped in what is known as the *Exodus*.

After the Hebrews established themselves in Palestine and prospered during the united monarchy under David and Solomon, the kingdom split into two parts: Israel and Judah. In a somewhat weakened condition these two kingdoms were subjected to the invasions or intrigues of several Egyptian monarchs. Probably in the year 925 B.C. Shishak I (Sheshonk I) of Egypt invaded Judah (1 Kings 14:25-26) and even marched into the territory of Israel, as archaeological discoveries show. About 700 B.C., in the days of King Hezekiah and the prophet Isaiah, Tirhakah of Egypt led an army into Palestine to help the Jews against invading Assyrians (2 Kings 19:9). Near the end of the seventh century B.C., Pharaoh Necho of Egypt led an army through Judah to come to the aid of weakened Assyria. When King Josiah tried to stop him, the Hebrew monarch lost his life (2 Kings 23:28-30). During the last days of the kingdom of Judah, while Nebuchadnezzar was besieging Jerusalem (588-86 B.C.), Pharaoh Hophra invaded Palestine in a vain effort to aid the Hebrews and defeat the Babylonians. Jeremiah predicted the Egyptians' destruction (Jeremiah 44:30).

After the destruction of Jerusalem, a group of Jews forced Jeremiah to go with them into Egypt (Jeremiah 43:6-7). During the centuries that elapsed between the Old and New Testaments, a very large and prosperous Jewish community arose in Egypt, especially in Alexandria. When the New Testament opened, Egypt again figured in the biblical narrative as the place of refuge for the holy family. There Joseph, Mary, and Jesus fled to escape the assassination attempts of Herod the Great (Matthew 2:13-23).

The biblical narrative is also often concerned with prophecies against Egypt. Ezekiel 29-32 represents one of the most extended prophecies against Egypt; but Isaiah, Jeremiah, Daniel, Hosea, Joel, and Zechariah also condemn the Egyptians. All prophecies concerning Egypt are not negative, however. In the midst of woe is the glorious prediction that Egypt shall be redeemed. In a future day a great spiritual revival shall sweep this land (Isaiah 19:19-25).

Since Egypt figures so significantly in the biblical narrative, there is no question but that she is a Bible land and therefore deserves attention here. Next to Palestine, more years of biblical history elapsed here than in any other country (a total of more than 430 years). And the influence of Egypt on Hebrew life crops up periodically, such as in the worship of the golden calf at Sinai and the calf worship instituted at Dan and Bethel by Jeroboam I of Israel after his brief exile in Egypt.

The Nile River

A vast desert plateau stretches across the entire width of North Africa from the Atlantic to the Red Sea and then continues on into central Asia. Two great river valleys interrupt this desert: the Tigris-Euphrates and the Nile. Of course, the focus here is on the latter. In fact, Egypt is the gift of the Nile, as the Greek historian Herodotus said in the fifth century B.C. Someone else has said that Egypt is the biggest and greenest oasis in the world. The absolute necessity of Nile waters to the maintenance of life in Egypt becomes clear from a quick glance at the rainfall statistics for the country. Along the Mediterranean at Alexandria, rainfall totals 6 to 8 inches per year; at Cairo it is 1½ to 2 inches; and south of Cairo it is less than an inch.

The Nile originates in equatorial Africa in the "Mountains of the Moon" (Mt. Ruwenzori), which pour their waters northward into Lakes Victoria, Albert, and Edward; these in turn become the sources of the Nile. The main source is Lake Victoria, which is supplied by tropical rains that fall almost daily. This huge lake covers about 27,000 square miles and is second only to Lake Superior among world lakes. From Lake Victoria to the Mediterranean, the distance is 2,450 miles in a straight line, but the Nile actually travels a distance of about 4,150 miles in a winding course and is the longest river in the world.

The branch of the Nile coming from these lake reservoirs is called the White Nile, even though its waters are grayish-green in color. It is light, however, by comparison with the Blue Nile, which is dark or turbid and carries much loose soil. The Blue Nile descends from the highlands of Abyssinia and joins the White Nile at Khartoum, about 1,350 miles in a straight line from the Mediterranean. Approximately 140 miles north of the union of the two Niles, the river receives its only other tributary, the Atbara. Both the Blue Nile and the Atbara are insignificant streams except in flood season.

The Nile flood was significant for the ancient Egyptian. It softened and watered the soil, washed salts out of it, and deposited a new layer of rich black loam. That had a considerable amount of humus already worked in, because the river torrents carried down vegetation from the Abyssinian highlands. It is estimated that the Nile has deposited at least ten feet of silt over the whole valley since 3,000 B.C.

The flood could be depended on to come at the same time every year. At the beginning of June, the river began to swell; between July 15 and 20 the increase was rapid and continued until the end of September. At that time, it ceased to rise and remained at a crest for 20 to 30 days. In October it rose again and attained its greatest height. Thereafter it gradually fell; and in January, February, and March, the fields dried off. Before the Aswan Dam was built in 1902, a low inundation meant famine; a high inundation would sweep away dikes and the mud-brick villages. An average rise at the turn of the century was 26 feet; only 21 feet would cause suffering or famine; 30 feet brought danger of a flood. So Egypt was precariously perched along the Nile.

There are six places in the Nile between Aswan and Khartoum where the river has failed to cut a clear channel through the stones, and rocks are piled in irregular masses in the streambed. The cataracts, as they are called, have no great or sudden falls as at Niagara; but they do present serious impediments to navigation. Even though it is a little tedious to recite the specifics of these cataracts, one cannot get any idea of their nature without some detail. The first cataract, at Aswan, was 3 miles long before construction of the low dam and had a fall of 16½ feet. The distance between the first and second cataracts is 214 miles; the second cataract itself is 124 miles long with a fall of 216 feet. From the second to the third cataract is a distance of 73 miles, and the third cataract is 45 miles long with a drop of 36 feet. Two miles farther upstream is the fourth cataract, which is 80 miles long and has a drop of 110 feet. In another 60 miles one encounters the fifth cataract, which is 100 miles long and has a drop of about 80 feet. Then one must travel 188 miles to reach the sixth cataract, which is 8 miles long and has a fall of 2 feet. North of Aswan the river is unimpeded because it no longer flows through sandstone; the limestone of northern Egypt is not so hard for the Nile to cut through.

Lower Egypt

Egypt consists of two lands: the trough of upper Egypt in the south and the spreading delta of lower Egypt in the north. The delta is a pie-shaped region formed by silt deposits of the Nile over the millennia. Roughly the equivalent of lower Egypt, it is about 125 miles from north to south and about 115 miles from east to west. In ancient times there were seven branches of the Nile in the delta, but these gradually silted up. Today two branches remain; the western is known as the Rosetta, and the eastern as the Damietta. In pharaonic times, Egyptians did not live in the northern delta in very large numbers. There were no important towns along the coast. Edfu, considered to be Egypt's most northerly town, was 30 miles inland. Before Alexander the Great founded the city to which he gave his name, only a small market town stood on the site. Greeks considered the Egyptian seaboard far from hospitable. At a very early period the Egyptians established observation posts to prevent pirates from entering the river mouths.

Along the eastern edge of the delta the Egyptians built defenses

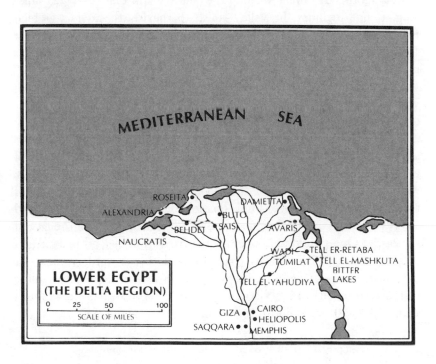

against Asiatic invaders. In the vicinity of these fortresses they established store cities or granaries with sufficient supplies for the Egyptian
garrisons. During the years that the Israelites were enslaved by the
Egyptians, they were forced to build store cities in this area (Exodus
1:11). No doubt the land of Goshen (Genesis 46:28—47:31) was located in the eastern delta in the area around the Wadi Tumilat, a valley
about 40 miles long connecting the Nile valley with Lake Timsah—
now a part of the Suez Canal. The fields to the north of the Wadi
Tumilat are among the richest in Egypt. Pithom was probably a town
in the Wadi Tumilat region, and Raamses was probably the rebuilt site
of Avaris.

The Nile Valley

The Nile valley is a tube, shut in on either side by cliffs and corked
up at the southern end by the cataracts. Egypt proper extended north
from the first cataract at Aswan. From Aswan to Cairo at the base of
the Delta is approximately 600 miles, and from Cairo to the Mediterranean is another 125 miles, making the country approximately 725 miles
long. If one includes the valley south to the fourth cataract, which
Egypt ultimately conquered, the length of the country was about
1,100 miles. The part of the valley between the first and sixth cataracts
is known as Nubia.

From cliff to cliff the Nile valley ranges from about 10 to 31 miles in
width between Cairo and Aswan. But the cultivated area is only about
6 to 10 miles wide along that stretch of the river and narrows to 1 or 2
miles in width around Aswan. This cultivated tract is only about 5,000
square miles. If one adds the most heavily populated southern part of
the Delta, ancient Egypt would approximate 10,000 square miles,
roughly equal to the state of Maryland or a little less than the area of
the country of Belgium. Thus the inhabited part of Egypt is and
always has been one of the most densely populated spots on the face of
the earth.[1] One should not conclude that irrigation or land reclamation
projects could add unlimited tracts of land to the verdant area, for
beyond the deposit of black loam (33 to 38 feet in depth) the soil is
marginal in quality. The Nile River north of Aswan has a maximum
width of 1,100 yards and narrows in places to about 550 yards. An

---

1. The cultivated part of Egypt in modern times is less than 14,000 square miles.

elaborate system of irrigation canals and reservoirs made possible a profitable agricultural program, and the wealth of Egypt became chiefly agricultural.

The valley is flanked on the west by cliffs of the Libyan tableland, which rise to approximately 1,000 feet. Beyond that rolls the Libyan desert, part of the great Sahara. West of the Nile extends a chain of oases, the largest of which is Fayum, about 55 miles southwest of Cairo. In the center of the Fayum is Lake Qarun, Egypt's only large inland lake, which today covers 90 square miles and is about 17 feet deep. It is surrounded by slightly less than a half million acres of good farmland. That area was especially developed during the Middle Kingdom (c. 2000-1800 B.C.) and under the Ptolemies (305-30 B.C.). On the east of the Nile, between the river and the Red Sea, rise granite mountains (to a height of 6,500 feet) with gold-bearing quartz veins and deposits of alabaster and semiprecious stones.

South of Aswan the granite mountains of Nubia (hardest in the world) confine the river. The quarries of Syene at Aswan are famous for their extremely hard and durable red granite. In Nubia the valley is only 5 to 9 miles wide, and the verdant area is very narrow, often consisting of only a melon patch. The river itself in the 200 miles between the first and second cataracts had an average breadth of about 1,650 feet. Much of that area is now completely changed by the construction of the High Dam at Aswan and the creation of Lake Nasser behind it.

Egypt As a Gift of the Nile

In a sense, it may be said that Egypt is the Nile. The Nile provided water to sustain life on a day-by-day basis, irrigating crops as well as laying alluvial silt on which to grow them.[2] The chief crops were barley, emmer, wheat (introduced in the Greco-Roman period), and

---

2. The climate of Egypt is subtropical. Blue skies, strong sunlight, and dry atmosphere are characteristics of the Nile valley. Mean temperatures for January and July, the coldest and hottest months, range as follows:

| | January | | July | |
	Max.	Min.	Max.	Min.
Alexandra	65°	50°	86°	71°
Cairo	65°	42°	100°	71°
Aswan	74°	48°	107°	79°

In Cairo the thermometer may go up to 113° in the summer, and in the valley it sometimes reaches 122°.

other grains not yet identified. The "corn" of which the King James Version speaks must be understood as an earlier English word for cereals, and should not be confused with the Indian corn that came from the New World to the Old in the sixteenth century. Onions, garlic, beans, lentils, and lettuce were common vegetables. Oil came from castor oil plants and sesame, rather than from the olive as in other Mediterranean lands. Honey was the chief sweetener, and barley beer the normal alcoholic drink. Grape wine was a luxury commodity. Domesticated animals included oxen, cattle, sheep, goats, donkeys, and horses. Among the fowl raised were pigeons, ducks, geese, and chickens (beginning in the Empire period, around 1500 B.C.). Linen clothing came from flax, likewise grown on the soil. Along the Nile grew papyrus reeds, from which a kind of "paper" could be made for writing purposes. And along the Nile was clay, from which could be made pottery and sun-dried bricks for the houses of the poor.

The river itself was an all-weather highway. One could float northward with the current and could sail southward against the weak current (3 miles per hour) by means of the prevailing northerly winds. Boats were made of papyrus bundles and sycamore wood. Trees from Nubian wadis gave the ancient Egyptians the wood for the barges that carried the huge loads of stone for construction of pyramids, temples, palaces, and other magnificent structures of the ancient period. Cedars of Lebanon also were imported for construction of Egyptian ships. In gratitude for all the Nile did for them, the ancient Egyptians deified the river and worshiped the Nile god, Hapi. It is clear, then, that the first of the ten plagues, which turned the Nile to blood, was more than a nuisance to the Egyptians. It was an attack on one of their gods, which demonstrated the superiority of the God of heaven.

Egyptian Isolation

The ancient Egyptians lived in comparative isolation and peace in their valley home. The cataracts on the south, the deserts on east and west, and the harborless coast of the Mediterranean protected them from invasion and left them free to develop a homogeneous culture. Chiefly at the two northern corners of the Delta, outside influences could sift in. There were Semitic incursions from the east and Libyans, possibly of European origin, from the west. Defenses were erected to protect against both. The security of their valley home and the regular provision of the sun and the Nile gave the Egyptians a sense of confidence and well-being that was not the lot of other peoples of the ancient Near East. They built their great capitals at Memphis (biblical Noph, near modern Cairo) at the Thebes (biblical No or No-Amon, 440 miles south of Cairo, at modern Luxor) and had no great upset of their way of life until the Hyksos domination about 1730 B.C. Though life was not destined to be quite the same thereafter, they gained a new sense of power and importance during the Empire period (c. 1580-1100 B.C.) "when Egypt ruled the East."

The Sinai

Egypt dominated the Sinai during most of her ancient history. This area was important for its copper and turquoise resources, the mining of which was apparently a government monopoly. But the Sinai has special significance in Scripture as the scene of Israel's wilderness wanderings and receipt of the law and pattern for building the Tabernacle—later to serve as a pattern for Solomon's Temple. Sinai is shaped like a wedge between Africa and Arabia and juts down into the Red Sea. The Gulf of Suez separates it from the African mainland, and the Gulf of Aqaba separates it from Arabia. Its northern shore fronts on the Mediterranean, and at the northeast it abuts on the land of Canaan. The peninsula is about 140 miles long.

Sinai is a rugged, waste region with a landscape of wild beauty and grandeur. The barren mountain ranges of red and gray granite and gneiss often have colorful veins of stone that look almost unreal. There is little settled population, and there are few oases to sustain human life. Less than one-tenth of one percent of the peninsula is currently under cultivation, and probably no more than that was farmed in ancient times.[3] Grazing grounds are also sparse. The population of the area today is around 200 thousand, and the Egyptian government is laying plans to increase that to 1 million by the year 2000. Informed observers doubt the feasibility of this effort however.

Traditionally Mount Sinai, where Moses received the law, is identified with Jebul Musa (mountain of Moses) in the southwest corner of

3. Efraim Orni and Elisha Efrat, *Geography of Israel*, 3d ed. rev. (Jerusalem: Israel U., 1971), p. 359.

the peninsula. This 7,519-foot peak is one of three major peaks that dominate a region of mountains at the southern tip of Sinai. There is an adjacent plain where the Israelites could have camped and where Bedouin today obtain water by digging shallow wells.

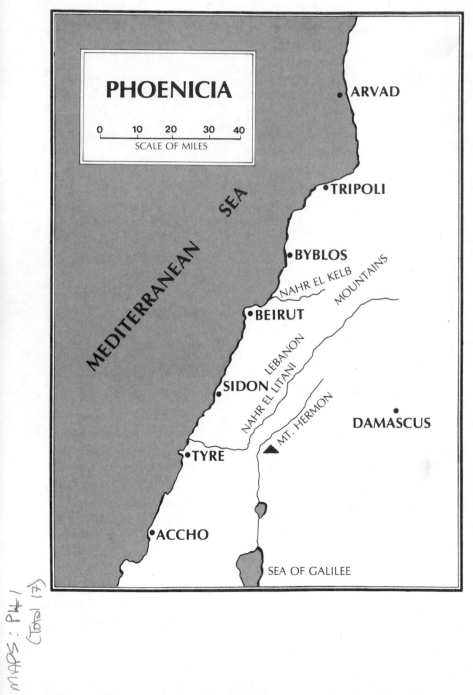

PHOENICIA

0   10   20   30   40
SCALE OF MILES

ARVAD

MEDITERRANEAN SEA

TRIPOLI

BYBLOS

NAHR EL KELB

MOUNTAINS

BEIRUT

LEBANON

NAHR EL LITANI

SIDON

MT. HERMON

DAMASCUS

TYRE

ACCHO

SEA OF GALILEE

4
Phoenicia

Phoenicia has a special appeal to some Bible students because of her role in furnishing Solomon with cedars and other materials for his magnificent Temple and palace. It is significant to others as a source of Baal worship, which flooded the kingdom of Israel in the days when Jezebel ruled as Ahab's queen. It serves yet others as a good example of the fulfillment of God's prophetic judgment on a pagan society, for Tyre and Sidon both fell under the condemnation of the prophets. Though small, Phoenicia played an important part in the biblical narrative—much greater than that suggested by any or all of those three functions. It also played a significant role in the affairs of the ancient world in general—as colonizer, disseminator of the alphabet, and ruler of Mediterranean waters for several centuries.

Phoenicia, along with Palestine, is commonly classified by geographers as a part of Syria. However, in many periods of history it has been politically separated from Palestine and Syria. For purposes of organization and simplification of treatment, Phoenicia, Palestine, and Syria are given separate consideration in this book.

During most of her history, Phoenicia occupied a strip of the Syrian coastal plain roughly compassed by the present north and south boundaries of Lebanon. But at her height she extended her control south to Mount Carmel and north to Arvad—a distance of some 200 miles. Nowhere is this coastal plain—opposite the Lebanon Mountains—more than 4 miles wide, and it averages little over a mile. It is known that the Phoenicians controlled part of the Lebanon Range because they possessed substantial timber resources in the cedar forests. How far inland their boundaries extended is not known; certainly they were largely shut up to the coastal plain. Ancient Phoenicia probably never exceeded in area more than half of modern Lebanon and therefore would have approximated the size of the state of Delaware or the country of Luxembourg.

The "Coastal Plain"

It is somewhat misleading to refer to a Phoenician "coastal plain," because it is far from being one continuous stretch of plain. Rather, it is a series of pockets of plains, separated by deep gorges cut by a dozen torrents rushing down from the mountains to the east. These plains came to be known for the principal cities located in them. For instance, on the south lay the Plain of Accho (or Acre), then the Plain of Tyre, followed by the Plain of Sidon (or Zidon) and the Plain of Beirut, and so on up the coast. None of these plains was very extensive. Sidon's was about 10 miles in length; Tyre's about 15; neither was more than about 2 miles in width.

Rivers

Fortunately for the inhabitants, the coastal plain was extremely fertile and well-watered. Average annual rainfall at Beirut is about 38 inches. The rivers that cross the plain on their way to the sea are no more than mountain torrents. Fall rains and melting snows of spring render them unfordable near their mouths, and no boat can survive in them. But the rivers did bring down new deposits of rich soil and plenty of water for irrigation. Most important of the rivers of Lebanon are the Nahr el Litani (ancient Leontes), which enters the sea about 5 miles south of Sidon; and Nahr el Kelb (Dog River, ancient Lycus), which flows into the Mediterranean about 7 miles north of Beirut.

Barriers to Communication

Not only did these mountain streams prove to be a hindrance to communication, at least at certain seasons of the year, but rocky spurs posed more effective barriers. In fact, during the centuries before man learned to modify the configuration of the land, it was difficult—in some places impossible—to follow the coast by land. At Nahr el Kelb, for instance, the mountains wash their feet in the ocean, forming a virtually impassable promontory. Although the natives were thus inconvenienced, they had a strategic position for intercepting invaders. And conquerors made a practice of carving inscriptions on the cliffs at the Dog River Pass after signal victories. A total of twelve inscriptions may be seen there—ranging in date from the time of the Egyptian, Assyrian, and Babylonian empires to the 1946 Lebanese inscription commemorating the evacuation of all foreign troops from the country. The Romans were the first to overcome the dangers of the precarious path of ancient times at Nahr el Kelb by building a road along the coast. They were also the first to build bridges over the river gorges of the region. The new Lebanese highway, completed in 1960 and made possible by blasting away cliffs there, leaves the visitor entirely unappreciative of the difficulty of moving through this area when Phoenicians ruled the coast. Ancient Phoenician city-states communicated with each other by ship.

Unpromising Shoreline

Since the Phoenicians were the finest sailors of antiquity, it is surprising that they had hardly a natural harbor to use as a maritime base. The coast is one of the straightest on the map, without a single deep estuary or gulf. The man-made harbors which played so important a part in antiquity are nearly all silted up. Only Beirut offers safe anchorage for large modern vessels, but there are facilities at Tripoli for tankers to pick up oil from the pipeline of the Iraq Petroleum Company.

Silting and the activities of conquerors, such as Alexander the Great, have also joined to the mainland islands on which Sidon and Tyre were originally built. Phoenicians preferred such island sites because they were convenient for shipping and easily defensible against attack. Other important cities of ancient Phoenicia included Accho (Acre, Roman Ptolemais), Berytus (Biruta in Egyptian, Biruna in Amarna Tablets, now Beirut), Gebal (Greek Byblos, modern Jubayl), Tripoli, and Arvad.

The Lebanon Mountains

To the east of the coastal plain lay the virtually impassable Lebanon Mountains. If the Phoenicians wanted to penetrate the interior, they usually had to wait until summer, then make their way along the beds of dried-up mountain streams. There were two places, however, that gave easy access to the interior: at Accho in the south along the Nahr al Muqatta (biblical Kishon) and at Tripoli in the north along the Nahr al Kabir. Understandably these became important trade routes of antiquity. Even today, with the aid of modern engineering, there are few roads that cross the Lebanons.

The Lebanon Mountains are part of the western ranges of Syria, which consist of a number of separate groups divided by river valleys. The northernmost are the Amanus Mountains (modern Alma Dag), which begin in the Anti-Taurus and extend south to the Orontes River. The second are the Nusairiyah Mountains, extending from the Orontes to Nahr al Kabir. Next come the Lebanons proper, bounded by the Nahr al Kabir (near modern Tripoli) and the Nahr el Litani (near Tyre), a distance of 105 miles. South of the Litani rise the mountains of Galilee.

The Lebanons are the highest, steepest, and largest of the western Syrian ranges. As already indicated, they are over 100 miles in length. Their width varies from about 35 miles in the north to 6 miles in the south. They have many peaks as high as 7,000 to 8,000 feet, and in the north a few peaks 10,000 feet or more. Geologically, the Lebanons are composed of upper and lower strata of limestone, with an intermediate layer of sandstone.

The name *Lebanon* is derived from a Semitic word meaning "to be white." This whiteness refers to the snowcapped peaks of these mountains, which retain their blanket of snow for several months of the year. Melting snows, augmented by spring rains, send hundreds of rivulets, some of considerable size, tumbling down the Lebanons toward the Mediterranean. Some of these rivers continue to flow throughout the year, and many of them have cut substantial gorges in the mountain chain.

While the western side of the Lebanons is well-watered and descends in a series of ledges to the Mediterranean, the eastern side is without substantial water supply and rises almost vertically from El

Bika, or "the valley," between the Lebanon and Anti-Lebanon Mountains.

Cedars of Lebanon

The Phoenicians, confined to a narrow plain by such formidable mountains, had to trade or die. They traded, becoming the finest mariners of antiquity. They were aided in their conquest of the sea by having some of the finest timber of the Near East at hand. The timber was not only of value to them for shipbuilding but was also sought after by neighboring monarchs for shipbuilding and construction of important buildings.

Egyptians, Assyrians, Hebrews, and others desired this valuable wood. Darius I, from faraway Persia, brought cedars of Lebanon for his winter palace at Susa (biblical Shushan). Bible readers are naturally most familiar with the Hebrews' use of cedar during the days of their greatest kings—a use made possible by David's and Solomon's alliances with Hiram of Tyre. David built a palace of cedar in Jerusalem after he captured the city from the Jebusites (2 Samuel 5:11; 7:2). Solomon built a palace largely of cedar, which must have been very beautiful indeed (for a description see 1 Kings 7). It is interesting to note in passing that it was called "the house of the forest of Lebanon." Best known of Hebrew structures built largely of cedar was Solomon's Temple, which was at least faced on the interior entirely with cedar (1 Kings 6:18). In the days of Solomon or soon after, cedar was extensively used in construction at Megiddo (one of the cities Solomon rebuilt and fortified), and perhaps at other cities as well. In the second Temple, Zerubbabel employed cedars of Lebanon (Ezra 3:7).

Best known of the remaining cedars is the stand near Besharreh, about 100 miles northeast of Beirut. This grove of four hundred trees is the most beautiful, the most ancient, and the most accessible to the modern tourist. It is located at an altitude of 6,300 feet. Another grove of about four hundred trees may be seen near Barook, southeast of Beirut, at an altitude of about 6,000 feet. The wind has twisted and stunted these. A third group of cedars is located near Hadet at 5,000 feet altitude, just a few miles west of the Besharreh stand. The Hadet group is more numerous than those of Besharreh, but not so beautiful. Cedars of Lebanon *(Cedrus Libani)* are also found on the Taurus and

Amanus Mountains in Turkey.

Cedars of Lebanon may live to be 1,500 years old, and about a dozen of those at Besharreh are over 1,000 years old. The youngest at Besharreh are said to be 200 years old. These cedars can reach a height of over 100 feet and a girth at the base of 40 to 45 feet. They may have a branch circumference of 200 or 300 feet. Their trunks are unusually straight; their branches are horizontal and shaped like fans. Cedarwood is hard, smooth, and reddish, and finds its chief protection in its bitter taste, which repels worms.

The cedar forests of ancient Phoenicia must have been extensive indeed, because extremely slow growth would have prevented substantial replacement of depleted stands of timber. In recent years reforestation efforts have resulted in some expansion of the number of cedars on the Lebanon Mountains. A grove of small trees may be seen near the Besharreh group. Cedar was not the only timber of ancient Phoenicia. Aleppo pine and cypress are still widely grown on the slopes of the Lebanons.

Phoenician Commerce

Confined as they were to the coastal plain, the Phoenicians became an important maritime people. After the fall of the Egyptian Empire (c. 1100 B.C.) and the lifting of Egyptian control over Phoenicia, the Phoenicians launched trade with Cyprus and thereafter with the Greek world. During the ninth century they moved into the western Mediterranean. Though they often acted as middlemen, native commodities also were important to their commercial development. As noted, cedars provided a valuable timber export, and the high quality murex (shellfish) along the seashore furnished an expensive purple dye. Applied to the wool produced from flocks of sheep pastured in the mountains, it helped to make possible the famous textile industry of the region. Craftsmen created fine furniture, jewelry, ivories, and metalware for export. Cedarwood provided the raw material for the furniture; copper and iron came primarily from Cyprus; silver from the Taurus Mountains; and ivory from elephants hunted in Syria. Exotic products such as myrrh and spices traveled from the south along the caravan routes to Damascus and thence to Phoenician cities. The Phoenicians' search for metals took them all the way to Spain, where they obtained copper and silver, and to which tin was brought from Cornwall in England.

As the Phoenicians engaged in their commercial exploits, they established trading posts or supply stations in Malta, Sicily, Sardinia, the Balaeric Islands, Utica, Carthage in North Africa, and Gadez (Cadiz) in Spain. Those points gradually developed into full-fledged colonies, so the Phoenicians found themselves to be exporters of people as well. And under the leadership of Carthage, those western dependencies contested with Rome for mastery in the western Mediterranean during the third and second centuries B.C.

Moreover, as the Phoenicians engaged in commerce, they exported the alphabet to the Greek world—at least by the middle of the eighth century B.C., and possibly much earlier. Though the alphabet is called Phoenician, the earliest alphabetic inscriptions presently known come not from Phoenicia, but from Palestine. Where and when the alphabet was invented is not certainly known, but the Phoenicians—with their widespread commercial contacts—were the transmitters of it to the West.

Tyre

Most important of the cities of Phoenicia from a biblical standpoint is Tyre. Here lived King Hiram, who had an extended involvement with David and Solomon; and here Paul spent a week with a group of Christians on the way back to Jerusalem from this third missionary journey (Acts 21:3-7). When Hiram took the reins of government, Tyre consisted of a small island about a half mile from the Phoenician coast, with a yet smaller island lying to the southwest. (Whether or not there was a Tyre on the mainland at the time is uncertain; at least it is commonly agreed that the island Tyre was founded earlier than the town on the mainland). Hiram joined these two islands and then claimed from the sea an area on the east of the larger island, making the total circumference of the island about 2½ miles. Then he proceeded to rebuild and beautify the temples; the most famous was the one to the god Melkart, which had long stood on the smaller island. Subsequently, attention was given to the harbors and fortifications of the city, the inhabitants constructing by means of piers the Sidonian harbor on the north and the Egyptian harbor on the south.

For centuries a mainland Tyre and an island Tyre stood side by side until Nebuchadnezzar of Babylon besieged the mainland city and destroyed it (585-572 B.C.). Unable to take the island city, he allowed it to continue. Then in 332 Alexander the Great attacked Tyre and engaged in a seven-month siege. To facilitate his conquest he determined to build a causeway 200 feet wide out to the island city and used the ruins of the mainland city to construct it. In the process, he scraped the mainland city as bare as the top of a rock and destroyed the island city as well. Thus, specific prophecies against the great metropolis were fulfilled (see Ezekiel 26:3-12, 14, 19; 28:21-23).

In time, sands drifted against Alexander's causeway and formed a peninsula where island and causeway had been. Later the city was rebuilt by non-Phoenician peoples and was again a thriving port by the time Paul arrived.

Excavations at Tyre conducted by the Lebanese Department of Antiquities have brought to light many exciting things. Most of the findings date to the Roman period and include an arena, a hippodrome some 500 yards long (one of the largest in the Roman world), an aqueduct, baths, a magnificent roadway (above which stands a monumental arch), and much more. Unfortunately most of the remains do not go back further than the second century B.C. It is not possible to reconstruct a picture of what Tyre was like when Paul was there, or of the nature of the place during Old Testament times. Almost certainly, the earlier periods at Tyre will never be known. Archaeology is very destructive, and there is no inclination to tear away all the striking remains now revealed at the site to see what lies beneath them.

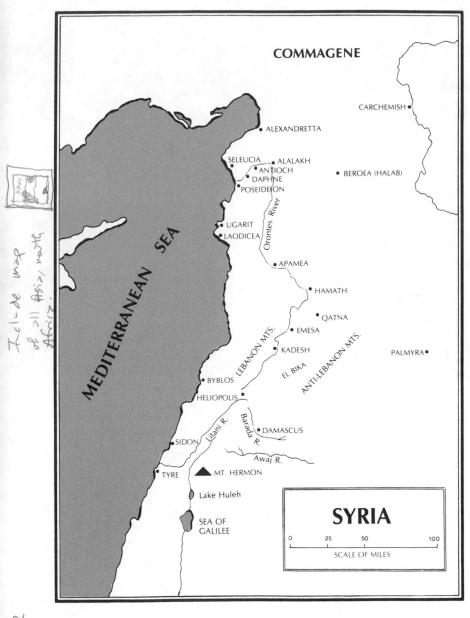

COMMAGENE

CARCHEMISH •

• ALEXANDRETTA

SELEUCIA
• ALALAKH
ANTIOCH
DAPHNE
• POSEIDEON

• BEROEA (HALAB)

Orontes River

• UGARIT
• LAODICEA

• APAMEA

• HAMATH

• QATNA

• EMESA

LEBANON MTS.

KADESH

PALMYRA •

EL BIKA

ANTI-LEBANON MTS.

MEDITERRANEAN SEA

• BYBLOS

HELIOPOLIS •

Litani R.

Barada R.

• DAMASCUS

• SIDON

Awaj R.

• TYRE

▲ MT. HERMON

Lake Huleh

SEA OF
GALILEE

SYRIA

0   25   50   100

SCALE OF MILES

5

Syria

Some have called Syria an international football, kicked around by the major powers surrounding her. Others have described her as a crossroads of civilization. However one looks at her, greater Syria has commonly been acted upon in history rather than acting upon her neighbors. The existence of a strong power in Asia Minor, Mesopotamia, or Egypt would mean aggressive action against Syria. With a strong power on both the northern and southern borders, Syria became a battleground. Sargon of Akkad, Hammurabi of Babylon, the Egyptians, Hittites, Assyrians, Chaldeans, Persians, Greeks, and Romans—each in their turn—conducted military campaigns there, sent in their cultural influences, or politically dominated the area.

Strategic Position

Syria has held too good a position for neighboring countries to ignore her. A land bridge between Asia and Africa, she naturally provided a route for conquering armies. Arteries of trade from Mesopotamia, Asia Minor, and Egypt converged on such cities as Damascus. Although the Syrian coast is not hospitable, throughout Syrian history people have been coming to and from it; and almost every town on the coast has had its heyday of maritime activity.

Wealth

Moreover, Syria had too many riches to be left to her own fate. There was the wealth of the forests, especially in the Lebanon region and north Syria. The cedars and cypresses of Lebanon, the Amanus Mountains, and the regions near Damascus, together with their resin and oil, were used in many countries. The wood and resin of the Syrian terebinth and sumac were likewise well-known. The laurel wood near Daphne was famous. Syrian figs were renowned, and olive culture was widespread, as was the culture of the vine. Plums, pears, apples, and dates produced in the area were much in demand, especially during the Roman period. Syrian wines were the only ones imported by all countries of the ancient world. Papyrus was also grown in Syrian fens and here as in Egypt was used as a writing material. One must not neglect to mention the products of medicinal and aromatic plants, which were a most important source of revenue for the country. Note especially the Syrian styrax (storax), nard, silphion (silphium), and magydaris. The vegetables of the area were apparently superior to those of Egypt. Damascus and Apamea were well-known Syrian centers of cattle breeding. The exploitation of the mineral wealth of the region in ancient times is not so widely known; but cinnabar, alabaster, amber, and gypsum were extensively produced in Syria.[1]

The Boundaries of Syria

The boundaries of Syria have fluctuated over the centuries according to political arrangements. When the power of the central government has been strong, it has exerted its control over the nomadic peoples of the desert; so the boundary line has moved east. When the central government has weakened, the nomads have pushed the boundary line westward. During the days of David and Solomon, the Hebrew kingdom virtually engulfed Syria. In days of Assyrian strength, the northern boundary of Syria was pushed southward. In days of Israelite weakness, Syrian kings were able to push their south-

---

1. For documentation and summary on the wealth of Syria, see especially F. M. Heichelheim, "Roman Syria," in *An Economic Survey of Ancient Rome*, ed. Tenney Frank (Baltimore: Johns Hopkins, 1938), 4:123-257, especially 127-40, 152, and 156.

ern boundary southward. When Seleucid kings ruled from Antioch (modern Antakya), they managed, at least temporarily, to control most of the old Persian Empire (including Phoenicia and Palestine). Roman provincial organization also gave Syria a rather large territory.

Originally *Syria* was a term that applied only to a powerful state whose center was in the Lebanon district and whose capital was Damascus. The Assyrians called this country west of the Euphrates "the Land of Amurrû." But geographers, following such ancient authorities as Strabo (who wrote during the lifetime of Jesus Christ on earth) and the Arab geographers, commonly consider the limits of Syria to be the Taurus Mountains and the Euphrates River on the north, the Sinai Desert on the south, and the Mediterranean Sea and the Syrian Desert on the west and east. Strabo divided Syria into four regions: Commagene (a district between the Taurus and the Euphrates), Seleucid Syria (the central section around Antioch and Latakia), Coele-Syria (including the valley between the Lebanon and Anti-Lebanon Mountains and much of southern Syria), and Phoenicia-Palestine.[2]

But biblical students—and many others as well—generally make a distinction between Syria and Palestine. Syria is restricted to the territory at the arch of the Fertile Crescent, bounded on the west by the Mediterranean, on the south by what became known as Galilee and Bashan, on the east by the Syrian Desert, and on the north by the Euphrates River and the Amanus Mountains. Sometimes it is considered to include Phoenicia. In this volume Syria is not generally used to include either Palestine or Phoenicia; separate sections are devoted to those areas. The southwest boundary is set at the Lebanon Mountains, which effectively shut off Syria from the coast.

Regions of Syria

Syria consists of a series of strongly marked zones—coastal plain, mountain ranges, valleys with luxuriant vegetation, and stony or sandy tracts in the east which are either desert or largely unproductive.

The coast of the eastern Mediterranean, 440 miles from Alexandretta to the Egyptian border, is one of the straightest in the world,

2. René Dussaud, *Topographie Historique de la Syrie Antique et Médiévale* (Paris: Paul Geuthner, 1927), pp. 1-2.

with no deep estuary or gulf and no protecting island of any size. However, at Carmel and northward, where hills approach the coast, short capes jut out and a few bays and islets have formed harbors sufficient for the ships of antiquity. In Syria proper there were small harbors at such places as Latakia (ancient Laodicea) and Ras Shamra (ancient Ugarit). Seleucia (the port for Antioch) was hardly more than a roadstead. The coastal plain, never more than a few miles wide, was largely inconsequential in Syrian history. Much of it is merely a broad strip of sand dunes covered by short grass and low bushes.

Overlooking the coastal plain is a line of mountains that begins with the Amanus Mountains in the north and extends all the way to the towering massif of Sinai in the south. The Amanus (rising to a height of some 5,000 feet) are a southward offshoot of the Tauric system. Separating Syria from Asia Minor, the Amanus range is cut on its southern fringe by the Orontes gorge and is crossed by roads to Antioch and Aleppo. The chief pass over the mountains is at Beilan, the Syrian Gates, at an altitude of 2,400 feet. South of the Orontes the range is continued by Jebel Akra ("the bald," classical Casius), which rises to a height of 5,750 feet and extends to Latakia, south of which it bears the name of Nusairiyah (Bargylus). The Nusairiyah chain is broken on the south by the Nahr el Kebeer (the Kebeer River), which today forms the border between Syria and Lebanon and to the south of which extend for 105 miles the Lebanon Mountains (with peaks over 10,000 feet).

Behind the western mountains range is a deep valley, a great fault extending from Armenia to the Gulf of Aqaba on the Red Sea and containing the deepest ditch on the earth's surface. One may start along this third topographical region of Syria in the neighborhood of Antioch, where the Orontes River turns westward to cut through the mountains to the sea. Here the plain is broad and extremely rich, none of it more than 600 feet above sea level. From Antioch the valley of the Orontes ascends slowly between the western range and the high plateau of northern Syria. At Hama (Hamath) the altitude is 1,015, and at Homs (ancient Emesa) it rises to 1,660 feet.

After Homs, the valley becomes El Bika (El Beqâ; "the cleft") between the Lebanon and Anti-Lebanon Mountains. Varying in breadth from 6 to 10 miles, El Bika rises around Baalbek (ancient Heliopolis) to over 3,770 feet. Here is the watershed; to the north flows the Orontes (246 miles long and largely unnavigable), and to the south flows the Litani (90 miles long). Both rivers eventually turn westward and flow into the Mediterranean. El Bika is some 75 miles long and always has been a rich agricultural and pastoral region. Its grazing land supports large flocks of sheep and goats. Its vines and other fruits flourish, and there is good wheatland. Here, as well as along the lower course of the Orontes, there are abundant ruins of ancient towns, testifying to the fact that this whole area was prosperous in ancient times—much more so than at present.

The eastern mountain range (Anti-Lebanon) constitutes the fourth topographical region of Syria. But it has no counterpart to the northernmost sections of the western mountain range. Rising from the Syrian plateau south of Homs, it opposes the Lebanons in almost equal length and height. This mountain complex is divided into two parts by the broad plateau and gorge of the Barada (biblical Abana) River. To the north is the Jebel esh Sherqi ("Eastern Mountain"), the uppermost ledge of which is a high plateau some 20 miles broad and about 7,500 feet high. It is a stony desert resting on a foundation of chalky limestone. Its western flank falls steeply to El Bika and is virtually uninhabited; the eastern side is more accessible.

The southern part of the eastern range, Jebel esh Sheikh, or Mount Hermon, rises to a height of 9,232 feet and is one of the highest and most majestic peaks of Syria. Here snow settles deep in winter and hardly disappears from the summit in summer. In contrast with the northern part of the Anti-Lebanons, Mount Hermon has more villages on its western slopes and fewer on its eastern.

On the south and east, the slopes of Hermon fall swiftly to the vast plateau of Hauran, the treeless surface of which is volcanic, and its soil a rich, red loam. The lava field covers an area almost 60 miles long by as many wide. On the east the Hauran is bounded by the mountain of Hauran, or the "Mountain of the Druzes." This bulwark is about 35 miles north and south and 20 miles east and west, with a summit that rises to 6,000 feet. In the north the Hauran is 2,000 to 3,000 feet above sea level, but in the south it shelves off to its limit in the deep valley of the Yarmuk. Known in classical times as Auranitis and in biblical times as Bashan, the Hauran has some of the best wheatland in the Near East. It was one of the granaries of the empire during the Roman period.

The Anti-Lebanons collect their waters and send them southward into the Jordan system and eastward far into the desert (Damascus is about 30 miles east of Hermon) in the channel of the Barada River. On a lofty and drainable plateau some 2,200 feet in altitude, the Barada has created 150 square miles of fertility, the Ghûtah, from which rises the city of Damascus, civilization's outpost in the desert. Though defenseless and on no natural line of commerce, Damascus has learned to exploit the fertility of her hinterland and to bend to herself much of the traffic between Egypt and Mesopotamia, as well as points west. In this way she has retained her prosperity over the centuries and today has a population of about 1,250,000. The Barada River (about 45 miles long) divides into five branches in the Damascus oasis and finally loses itself in the desert. Another river that rises in the Anti-Lebanons is the biblical Pharpar, identified with the Awaj, which flows some distance south of Damascus and disappears in swamps east of the city. Naaman was immensely proud of both these life-giving rivers of his homeland (2 Kings 5:12).

East of the Hauran Plateau and its boundary of Jebel ed Druz lies the Syrian Desert, which is a continuation of the great Arabian Desert. The Syro-Iraqi Desert forms a huge triangle whose base rests on the Gulf of Aqaba on the west and the Gulf of Kuwait on the east, and whose apex reaches toward Aleppo on the north. At its widest, this desert stretches about 800 miles.

Trade Routes

Numerous trade routes crossed the sands of Syria. A Transjordanic route led from the Gulf of Aqaba to Petra and from there to Damascus. A coastal route ran from Gaza to Carmel, crossed Esdraelon, and in Galilee divided into branches, one to Damascus and the other north along the Orontes. The northern road to Mesopotamia led from Damascus north and passed through Homs (ancient Emesa), Arabian Haleb (Aleppo; ancient Beroea), and then east down the Euphrates River. Another link between Syria and Mesopotamia by a more southerly track took off from Damascus or Homs and proceeded by way of Palmyra (ancient Tadmor; 2 Chronicles 8:4) to ancient Dura-Europos. In the days of the Sino-Roman world peace (first and second centuries

A.D.), the Aleppo Road formed the last stage of the "silk route" from the Yellow Sea to the Mediterranean.

Climate

It seems that the climate of Syria has changed since New Testament times. Large sections of areas which are now mere desert were former- ly cultivated. East of Homs, where there is now not a green leaf nor a drop of water, the heavy basalt slabs of former oil presses are found in quantities.[3] But it is not clear how much of the change is related to rainfall and to what extent the change is due to lack of water regulation brought about by erratic political conditions.[4] The Syrian summer is hot and long (May to September), its winter short and mild. But there is considerable regional variation. Rainfall on the western mountain slopes and in the north of Syria is adequate. The eastern slopes have less precipitation. While Latakia on the coast enjoys over 30 inches of rainfall per year, the average at Damascus is about 9 inches and at Aleppo approximately 18 inches. Most of the population of the coun- try lives in areas where the average winter temperature is 42° to 43° F., the average summer temperature 83°, and the average annual tempera- ture 61° to 63°. These figures apply to both Aleppo and Damascus and would include many of the towns of interior Syria.

Antioch

Of course the most prominent of all Syrian cities during the Roman period was Antioch, the capital. Third city of the Empire after Rome and Alexandria, it has frequently been estimated to have sported a population of about a half million during the first century A.D.

The prosperity of Antioch came in part from her political position, in part from the arteries of commerce that flowed through her, and in part from the commodities produced there. Among the luxury goods that one could purchase there were fine leather shoes, perfume, spices,

---

3. Theodor Mommsen, *The Provinces of the Roman Empire from Caesar to Diocletian*, trans. William P. Dickson (New York: Scribner's, 1906), 2:148.
4. M. Cary, *The Geographic Background of Greek and Roman History* (Oxford: Clarendon, 1949), p. 165.

textiles, jewelry, books, and products of goldsmiths and silversmiths, who had held first place among the city's craftsmen ever since its founding.

Antioch was destined to become a great center of Christianity. It was the birthplace of foreign missions; all three of Paul's missionary journeys were launched from there (Acts 13:1-4; 15:35-36; 18:23). Disciples of Jesus were first called Christians there (Acts 11:26); and it was among the Antiochians that the question of Gentile relation to the Mosaic law first arose, with the resultant decision at the Jerusalem Council that Gentiles were not under the law (Acts 15).

Because of its Hellenistic foundation, Antioch enjoyed all the advantages of scientific city planning that men of that age desired. The area had a healthful climate, an adequate water supply, good drainage, fertile land, and many commercial advantages. Moreover, a city located at this spot (about 20 miles from the Mediterranean on the Orontes River) was far enough from the sea for protection and close enough for easy communication.

In this part of Syria the limestone is fissured, containing underground caverns and reservoirs in which collects the water that falls during the winter rainy season. Faults in the limestone produce springs that flow all year. Thus numerous springs were available for a new city foundation. That was especially true of the plateau of Daphne, some 5 miles southwest of Antioch. That plateau, roughly square in shape and measuring about 2,000 yards on a side, averaged about 300 feet above the level of the city. As a result, water from its springs could easily be carried by gravity through aqueducts to the city. In ancient times, five springs served the double function of watering the surface of the Daphne Plateau and supplying water for Antioch.

Antioch enjoyed a benign climate. A regular breeze blew daily from the sea up the Orontes River. This steady stream of fresh, cool air was especially welcome during the summer months, when it brought relief from high temperatures. The streets of the city were carefully oriented so the main thoroughfares caught the breeze as it blew up the valley. So pleasant were summers at Antioch that it became a popular vacation spot for people from Egypt and Palestine, as well as native Syrians.

The neighborhood was rich. A vast, open, fertile plain spread to the north of the city; and an abundance of grain, fruits, and vegetables grew there. Good stands of timber were available in nearby forests.

Good building stone could be quarried in the adjoining mountains. Plenty of fish could be obtained in the Lake of Antioch, which lay about twleve miles northeast of the city, and in the Mediterranean Sea.

As to commercial advantage, the Orontes Valley at Antioch opened into the plains of north Syria, across which passed the regular land routes from Iran and Mesopotamia to the Mediterranean. So it became a terminus of the caravan route from the East. And the Orontes was navigable as far as Antioch. Moreover, the city controlled the north-south road that joined Palestine, Syria, and Asia Minor.

Because of these advantages, the site of Antioch appealed greatly to Hellenistic city planners. Seleucus I founded the city under the northern slopes of Mount Silpius (which rises some 1500 feet above the plain) in May of 300 B.C. The first settlers were Macedonian soldiers and Athenian colonists. The people of Antioch traced the greatness of their city to their Attic origin.

The Seleucids also built a magnificent harbor for Antioch at Seleucia, about 5 miles north of the Orontes on the Mediterranean. Above this principal harbor of the coast Mount Pieria rises from the sea in a series of ledges. The lower city with the harbor and warehouses stood on a level about 20 feet above the quay. Above the lower city on a much higher shelf perched the upper city. The elevation displayed to best advantage the magnificence of the public buildings and temples of the city and made it a worthy gateway to an affluent kingdom. The sight must have been an impressive one to the apostle Paul as he sailed toward this port of Antioch at the end of his first missionary journey. However, it was not necessary to disembark at Seleucia. The Orontes was navigable as far as Antioch up to the time of the Crusades.

TEXT:

MAPS II
(P. 1962)

6

Iran

That Iran is a biblical land is clear from the fact that several Old Testament books are closely linked to Iran and Iranian affairs. The book of Ezra takes as its reference point decisions of Persian kings Cyrus, Darius, and Artaxerxes concerning return of the Hebrews from captivity. Nehemiah was cupbearer at the court of the Persian king Artaxerxes, and from the court he sallied forth to rebuild the walls of Jerusalem. The story of Esther took place in and around the Persian court. In addition, Haggai, Zechariah, and Malachi relate history that took place during the Persian period. Moreover Isaiah and Daniel prophesied concerning Persian affairs.

Persia is the anglicized form of *Parsis*, or *Pars*, the section of Iran adjacent to the Persian Gulf. Native Persians have always used the term *Iran* to designate their indefinitely bounded country. And this has been the official name of the country since 1935. The modern name *Iran* is derived from the ancient *Ariana*, meaning "the country of the Aryans." The Aryans were various Indo-European peoples who settled during prehistoric times in areas north and east of the Persian Gulf.

Geographically, *Iran* is an inclusive term referring to the large plateau between the plain of the Tigris on the west and the Indus River valley to the east. On the south it is bounded by the Persian Gulf and the Indian Ocean, and on the north by the Caspian Sea and chains of mountains that extend eastward and westward from the south end of the Caspian Sea.

Geographical Areas

In the days of the Persian Empire, Iran was divided into geographical and political areas as follows: At the north end of the Persian Gulf was Susiana, with its main center at Susa (biblical Shushan). North of Susiana in the interior was Media, the chief city of which was Ecbatana (modern Hamadan). Hyrcania (Asterabad) occupied a narrow strip of land south of the Caspian Sea. East of Susiana along the Persian Gulf was Persia with its leading royal cities of Persepolis and Pasargadae. North of Persia in the interior was Parthia. Gedrosia stretched along the Indian Ocean. It was bounded on the northwest by Drangiana and on the northeast by Arachosia. North of these two regions stretched Aria; and north of that, Bactria.

The Plateau

The plateau of Iran averages 3,000 to 5,000 feet in altitude. Over one-half of the drainage of the plateau flows inward to form inland lakes and sterile swamps. In its central region lie the great sand and salt deserts of Dasht-i-Lut and Dasht-i-Kavir. This continuous desert region stretches northwest to southeast about 800 miles in length and varies from 100 to 200 miles in width.

At the western edge of the plateau rise the Zagros Mountains with several peaks over 10,000 feet. This range is over 600 miles in length and 120 miles in width. It consists of numerous parallel folds enclosing fruitful valleys where wheat, barley, and other grains and fruits grow. South of the Caspian Sea stand the Elburz Mountains, the highest peak of which is Mount Damavand, about 60 miles northeast of Tehran. It is a conical peak 18,934 feet high, which was once volcanic. Damavand (or Demavend) is thought to be the Mount Bikni mentioned in Assyrian documents before 800 B.C. as the farthest point to which Aryans were chased by the Assyrian kings. To the northwest, the Iranian Plateau is united by the highlands of Armenia with the mountains of Asia Minor. To the northeast, the plateau is linked by the mountains of Khurasan (or Khorasan) and the Hindu Kush Range to the Himalayas. The total area of the plateau is over one million square miles, more than one-third the size of the forty-eight contiguous United States.

Rainfall

Iran is a country singularly lacking in rainfall. Only on the plain south of the Caspian and on the Elburz Mountains and Zagros Mountains is rainfall abundant. At Resht, precipitation is over 56 inches per year. But south of the Elburz at the national capital of Tehran, the figure drops to 9 inches. Farther south in the interior rainfall is about 2 inches per year. At the head of the Persian Gulf it annually measures about 10 inches.

Resources

Iran is primarily an agricultural and stockbreeding country. The northwestern part of the country, Azerbaijan, has fertile valleys with sufficient rainfall for growing various kinds of grain and fruits and vegetables. Agriculture prospers on the plain between the Caspian Sea and the Elburz Mountains, as it does in the fertile valleys of the mountains of Khurasan. The latter constitute the granary of Iran.

But Iran also possessed rich mineral resources. Its quarries provided marble, and its mountain slopes yielded building woods for the Sumerian princes as early as the third millennium B.C. Gold, iron, copper, tin, and lead were exploited early and especially attracted the attention of the Assyrians. Sargon of Akkad was interested in the wealth of the region 1500 years earlier, however. The oil deposits, so important to Iran's economy today, did not, of course, have any importance for ancient peoples.

Extent of Empire

The Medo-Persians cooperated with the Babylonians and Scythians in destroying the Assyrian Empire in 612 B.C. At that time they controlled an area in the western part of modern Iran. Subsequently, in 559 B.C., Cyrus, a Persian, later called the Great, rebelled against his Median overlord and established the Achaemenid dynasty. He went on to add Asia Minor and Mesopotamia to Medo-Persian holdings and died fighting to expand his borders in the east. His successor, Cambyses (530-522 B.C.), added Egypt to the Empire, and Darius I (521-486 B.C.) expanded holdings in the East and moved across the Hellespont into

Greece. Although the Greeks were able to repel the Persians, the latter created the greatest empire of Western Asia up to that time. It was more than 3,000 miles in extent from east to west and stretched from the Indus River in India to the Mediterranean and also included Asia Minor and part of Greece. A great postal road connected the biblical cities of Susa in western Iran and Sardis in western Asia Minor, a span of 1,500 miles.

Some Great Imperial Cities

Hamadan is the modern city that occupies the site of ancient Ecbatana, about 180 miles southwest of Tehran, high in the Zagros Mountains of western Iran. Cyrus made it his summer capital and apparently from this site issued the decree allowing the Jews to return to Jerusalem and build the Temple. This may be determined from the fact that in the palace there Darius I later found the scrolls of Cyrus containing this authorization. Ezra 6:2 gives the name of the place as Achmetha, the Aramaic form of Ecbatana. The city had been the capital of the Medes before Cyrus's revolt. A magnificent palace and fortress once stood there, remains of which archaeologists have discovered in the northeastern part of the modern city.

Cyrus established his main capital at Pasargadae, however. That city was located 30 miles northeast of the later royal center at Persepolis and is said to have been founded by him on the site of his victory over Astyages the Mede. The royal complex seems to have consisted of several pavilions set among gardens and surrounded by a masonry wall. Two tombs of Cyrus are shown there, one north of the palace and one in a Muslim cemetery west of the town.

Darius I constructed a great center at Persepolis soon after his accession in 521 B.C. It was not a capital in the political sense but a magnificent ceremonial shrine especially dedicated to celebration of the Persian New Year festival. At Persepolis, Darius built a large stone platform forty feet high, covering thirty-three acres. On this he erected several impressive structures, some of which scholars have not yet determined how to interpret.

But it is possible to identify the palace of Darius, with its main hall measuring 50 feet square; a large audience hall, begun by Darius and completed by Xerxes, the so-called *Apadana*, 197 feet square; the throne hall known as "the Hall of One Hundred Columns," started by Xerxes and finished by Artaxerxes, the central unit of which measured 225 feet square; and the treasury. North of the city, at Naksi-i-Rustam, are remarkable tombs cut into the rock of the cliffs for Darius and successive Persian rulers.

Susa, at the foot of the Zagros Mountains, some 150 miles north of the Persian Gulf, became the winter capital of the Persian Empire in the days of Darius I. This city is called *Shushan* in the Old Testament (Nehemiah 1:1; Esther 1:2; Daniel 8:2). Since this was the winter capital, we know that the story of Esther took place during the winter, as did Nehemiah's conversation with King Artaxerxes about the rebuilding of the walls of Jerusalem. Excavations reveal that Darius I began construction of the royal palace at Susa and that the main plan included three courts surrounded by large halls and apartments. The glory of these magnificent Persian centers came to an end when Alexander the Great swept through Persia in 331 B.C., looting and destroying. *Sic transit gloria!*

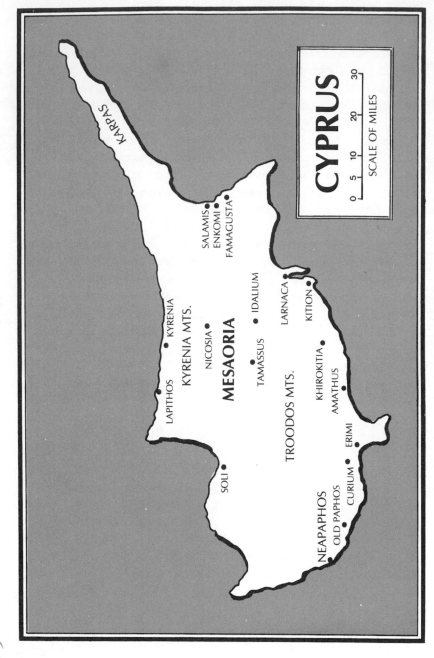

CYPRUS

SCALE OF MILES

0   5   10   20   30

KARPAS

SALAMIS
ENKOMI
FAMAGUSTA

LARNACA
KITION
IDALIUM

KYRENIA
KYRENIA MTS.
NICOSIA
MESAORIA
TAMASSUS

KHIROKITIA
AMATHUS

TROODOS MTS.

LAPITHOS

SOLI

ERIMI
CURIUM
OLD PAPHOS
NEAPAPHOS

MAPS C 1
(Total 21)

7

Cyprus

When Barnabas and Saul (later called Paul) sailed out of Antioch (perhaps in A.D. 45) to begin their first great missionary journey, their initial stop was on the island of Cyprus.[1] The island was the home of Barnabas and possessed a large Jewish population that needed to be reached with the Christian gospel. Hence there was a double appeal for the apostolic pair to engage in ministry there. Apparently they had considerable success—even the Roman governor made a profession of faith.

Barnabas and Saul landed at Salamis, the largest city of Cyprus (with perhaps 100,000 population), and apparently made a rather complete tour of the island, finally sailing from Paphos to Asia Minor. The Romans had constructed roads along both the northern and southern coasts from Salamis to Paphos, where they maintained the capital of this island province and where the governor lived. Whether Barnabas and Saul took a northerly or southerly route to Paphos or whether they took an alternate route through the interior we do not know. Estimates of how long the evangelists ministered on Cyprus vary from two to four months (see Acts 13:3-13). But this was not the end of missionary attention to the people of Cyprus. Later Barnabas took John Mark with him to Cyprus and continued to preach there for an indefinite period of time (Acts 15:39).

---

1. Old Testament references to Kittim or Chittim (e.g. Genesis 10:4; Numbers 24:24; Isaiah 23:1) commonly are identified with Cyprus.

Location and Size

Cyprus is the third largest island of the Mediterranean Sea. Exceeded in size only by Sicily and Sardinia, it has an area of 3,572 square miles. Located in the extreme northeast corner of the Mediterranean, Cyprus can be seen from both Asia Minor and Syria on a clear day. The former distance is about 43 miles and the latter about 60. Between Egypt and Cyprus the distance is about 250 miles. It is therefore easy to see why cultural influences from Asia Minor and Syria were felt on Cyprus long before those of Egypt.

Cyprus is sometimes likened to a silhouetted wheelbarrow being pushed along. The long Karpas Peninsula represents the handles, and the Akrotiri Peninsula to the south, the wheels. In ancient times it was compared to a deerskin or bullock's hide spread out on the ground. The tail is represented by the Karpas Peninsula, and the legs by four large promontories. The greatest length of the island is 138 miles and the greatest width 60 miles. Subtracting the approximately 40-mile-long Karpas Peninsula, Cyprus averages some 90 to 100 miles in length. The total coastline is 486 miles.

Mountains

The surface of Cyprus is almost evenly divided between mountain and plain. The mountains divide into two ranges: the Kyrenia, or Northern, Range and the Troodos Range. The gray-pink limestone Kyrenia Range extends along the whole of the northern coast some 3 miles from the coast and rises from 2,000 to 3,000 feet. Highest of the several peaks of this range is Akromandra, 3,357 feet in altitude. Conveniently, three gaps pierce this range: Panagra in the west, Kyrenia in the center, and Akanthou in the east. The Kyrenia Range tends to force the moisture from the vapor-laden winds from the north, providing sufficient moisture for the fertile coastal plain. The seaward slopes of the Kyrenia Mountains are profusely covered with trees (especially olive in modern times), shrubs, and flowers; the southern slopes are often bare. Most of the southern half of Cyprus consists of a confusion of steep-sided mountain ridges, array in such tangled profusion that it is almost impossible to discover any backbone or watershed. Several of the peaks of these Troodos Mountains rise more than 4,500 feet. The

highest is Chionistra, or Olympus (6,404 feet). White limestone plateaus occupy the area south of the Troodos massif. These fall in
steplike fashion as they approach the coast. In places they become sea
cliffs, but occasionally they recede to allow coastal plains with quite
rich alluvial soil.

The Central Plain

Between the two mountain ranges lies the broad plain of Mesaria, or
Mesaoria, some 60 miles long by 30 miles broad. Nicosia, the modern
capital of Cyprus, is located in the center of this plain. The granary of
the island, this plain also produces substantial quantities of vegetables
and fruit. Though now treeless except for a few recently planted trees,
Mesaria was in ancient times heavily forested. Through this plain once
flowed the two chief rivers of Cyprus—the Pedias (ancient Pediaeus)
and Yalias (ancient Idalia) to dump their waters into the Mediterranean
near ancient Salamis on the east coast. Reservoirs now tap their water,
and the stream beds are dry.

Rainfall and Climate

Rainfall occurs primarily during the months of December to February, but the amount is not large. The main agricultural areas receive
only 12 to 16 inches per year. Even this amount comes irregularly, and
severe droughts occur on the average of every 10 years. And since high
evaporation involves considerable loss, the supply of water constitutes
a serious problem. In recent years, just before Cyprus gained its independence (1960), British efforts at building dams, expanding irrigation,
and initiating reforestation considerably improved the water supply
and crop production of the island. While it is hoped that desalinization
plants may some day make possible an agricultural revolution on
Cyprus, the process of desalting ocean water is still too expensive to
permit the general use of water obtained in this way.

Prolonged drizzling from gray skies is rare in Cyprus even during
the rainy season—when the sun usually shines for at least some part of
every day. The mean temperature of the lowland areas in the coldest
months is approximately 50°-54° F.; for the hottest month it ranges
from 80° to 84°. The climate is very healthful, and the death rate is one

of the lowest in the world. The growing season roughly corresponds with the rainy season, and crops are harvested by March or April. During the summer and early fall, when there is rarely any rainfall, the fields give an appearance of aridity.

Forests

Forests were once one of the main resources of Cyprus; and the timber, so important for shipbuilding, was much sought after by the ancient imperial powers of the Mediterranean area. Actually, however, more trees were felled for copper and silver smelting than for shipbuilding. Eratosthenes, Greek astronomer and geographer of the third century B.C., talks of the plains as being "formerly full of wood run to riot, choked in fact with undergrowth and uncultivated."[2] The famous cedars have almost disappeared, but there are considerable stands of Aleppo and black pine. The main state forests today occupy a good part of the Kyrenia Range, the Karpas Peninsula, and the Troodos mass. State forests fill a total of 608 square miles, and there are also private and communally owned forests. Under the direction and protective hand of the Forest Department, timber and naval supplies may assume once again an important place in the economy of Cyprus.

Mineral Deposits

More important than timber to the economy of Cyprus in antiquity was her production of copper. In fact, so extensive was the island's export of this mineral that copper obtained its name from the name of Cyprus. The English word *copper* is derived from the Greek name of the island, Kypros, through the Latin *cuprum*. Produced as early as the third millennium B.C.,[3] copper has continued to be mined extensively until very recently. The island's copper, which was shipped all over the Mediterranean world in ancient times in the form of both ore and ingots, came from the foothills of the Troodos, especially along the southern coast and at Tamassus, southwest of Nicosia. To gain some understanding of the extent of the copper deposits on Cyprus and the extent of trade in the commodity over the millennia, it might be

2. Eratosthenes, *Excerpta Cypria*, trans. Claude D. Cobbam (Cambridge: U. Press, 1908), p. 3.
3. N. G. L. Hammond, *A History of Greece to 322 B.C.* (Oxford: Clarendon, 1959), p. 25.

helpful to note that Cypriot copper exports during the fiscal year ending in 1960 totalled 430,000 long tons.[4] However, at the present writing, known deposits have been virtually exhausted.

Though iron was mined on Cyprus in antiquity, the extent is in question. In modern times iron production often has far outstripped copper production. Gold and silver also were mined on the island in ancient times. The mining of silver there is thought to account for the large issues of silver coinage in the Ptolemaic Age.[5]

It is evident, then, that Cyprus had valuable resources during the first Christian century. And under an efficient Roman administration and the Roman peace the island achieved a relatively high level of prosperity. This prosperity was enhanced by the fact that a great shrine to Aphrodite, the Greek goddess of love and beauty, near the capital of Paphos brought numerous pilgrims to the island. Each spring a three-day festival to Aphrodite drew great crowds from all parts of Cyprus and surrounding countries. According to legend, Aphrodite was born at sea near Cyprus and floated in a shell to a spot near Paphos. Cyprus's some half million people, among them innumerable devotees of Aphrodite and thousands of Jews, provided a tremendous missionary challenge to Barnabas and Paul as they preached their way across the island.

4. *Britannica Book of the Year, 1961*, s.v. "Cyprus."
5. George Hill, *A History of Cyprus* (Cambridge: U. Press, 1940), 1:10.

Paul's Journeys

| 1 | 2 | 3 |

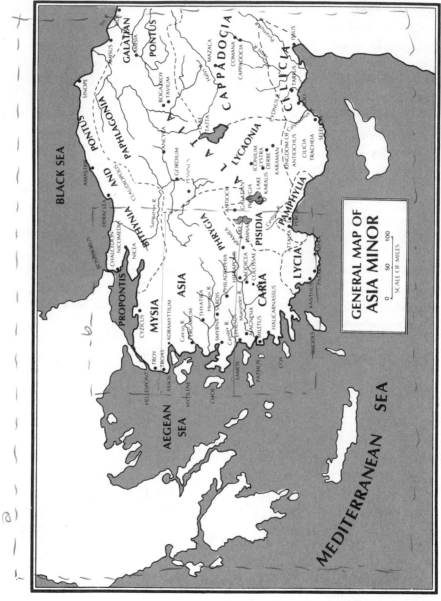

GENERAL MAP OF
ASIA MINOR

0   50   100
SCALE OF MILES

BLACK SEA

AEGEAN SEA

MEDITERRANEAN SEA

PONTUS

GALATIAN

PAPHLAGONIA

BITHYNIA AND PONTUS

CAPPADOCIA

CILICIA

LYCAONIA

PHRYGIA

GALATIA

PISIDIA

PAMPHYLIA

LYCIA

CARIA

ASIA

MYSIA

PROPONTIS

KINGDOM OF ANTIOCHUS

MAPS AVTS
(TOTAL 26)

8

Asia Minor

Main arteries of civilization converged on this important peninsula of the eastern Mediterranean world. At an early time peoples and ideas moved in from the Mesopotamian valley. From this center, men migrated to Crete, the Aegean islands, and even the Greek mainland. Waves of Greeks washed onto her shores during the first millennium B.C. During the same millennium Etruscans probably sailed from her western coasts to Italy, Persians swept across her plateaus into Greece, Alexander's hosts conquered her on the way to deal with the Persian king, and his Hellenistic successors established flourishing centers here. These cities enjoyed new heights of prosperity under the Roman peace during the first and second centuries A.D.

Not only was this peninsula important for the flow of population and culture in ancient times, it was also important to the advance of Christianity. Paul, the great apostle of Christianity, was born at Tarsus and in his missionary activities ranged over the entire length of Asia Minor. Subsequently, Peter seems to have preached in the northern and central portions of the peninsula. And the apostle John spent the last decades of his life ministering in the populous cities of the province of Asia. Altogether at least thirty-five towns, provinces, and islands adjacent to Asia Minor figure in the New Testament narrative.

Asia Minor is the general geographical term for the peninsula that forms the bulk of modern Turkey. Not in use in classical times, the descriptive seems to have arisen in the fifth century A.D. Anatolia commonly applies to that part of the peninsula west of the Halys River but frequently is used virtually as a synonym for Asia Minor.

Asia Minor is bounded on the north by the Black Sea, on the west by the Aegean and the straits of the Bosporus and Dardanelles, on the south by the Mediterranean Sea, and on the east by a line running northeastward from below the Gulf of Iskenderun to the Euphrates and up that stream to the Coruh (Chorokh) River and then to the Black Sea. The total area of the peninsula approximates 200,000 square miles, equal to that of New England, New York, New Jersey, Pennsylvania, Delaware, Maryland, and West Virginia.

The Central Plateau

The mass of Asia Minor is a plateau 3,000 to 5,000 feet above sea level, tilted down toward the north and west. Extensive and irregular, this plateau is fringed on all sides by higher mountain ranges; but on the west the hills are fewer and less imposing. While the plateau consists largely of rolling upland, it is diversified by highland massifs and numerous sunken basins occupied by lakes and marshes. Although the rivers entering the interior plains from the adjoining mountains in modern times are largely swallowed up in salt lakes and swamps, in New Testament times their waters were used for irrigation and helped to support many large cities. The surface of the northern part of the plateau is deeply eroded; in many places there are precipitous valley walls and rugged hillsides.

As a whole, the central plateau has slender resources. Because of its enclosed nature, much of the plateau is arid. It supports little plant or animal life and is used for grazing of sheep. It was not until the Hellenistic and Roman periods that town life developed there, and even then the larger towns were strung out along the edge rather than across the heart of the tableland.

The Mountain Ranges

As already noted, the central plateau is surrounded by mountain ranges. The Armenian mountains extend westward and fork near the eastern boundary of the peninsula into two ranges—the Taurus on the south and the mountains of Pontus on the north. The northern rim of mountains rises to about 9,000 feet, and the southern to 10,000 feet. Both consist of a series of overlapping ridges which permit only a few narrow and tortuous passages between the coast and the interior. East and northeast of the main Taurus system and parallel to it lies the Anti-Taurus Range.

Along the southeast edge of the plateau for a distance of about 150 miles rise groups of volcanic peaks. At the northeast end of this range stands Mount Erciyas Dagi (ancient Argaeus) to a height of 12,848 feet, the highest point in Asia Minor. Here in western Cappadocia, fertilized by lava dust and supplied with snow waters in summer, were fine orchards and the best horse pastures of the Near East, on which a strain of racers for the Roman circus was bred.

From the Phrygian mountains to the west of the central plateau extend mountain ranges—the Temnos, Boz Dag (ancient Tmolus), and Messogis—which delimit respectively the valleys of the Caicus, Gediz (ancient Hermus), and Menderes (ancient Meander). Since these valleys run east and west, they naturally conduct traffic in those directions. Thus, the only open face of Asia Minor is toward the west and northwest, where the plateau ends in a staircase down to the piedmont country. Since the western shore is easily accessible, most invasions of Asia Minor that have had lasting results have been launched from Europe (e.g., Phrygians, Greeks, and Galatians).

As intimated, the mountains of Asia Minor constitute formidable barriers, but there are strategic passes. The most important was, of course, the Cicilian Gates north of Tarsus. Two passes made possible routes from Antalya (biblical Attalia) to Laodicea and to Pisidian Antioch or Apamea. Another gave passage between Seleucia in western Cilicia to Karaman (ancient Laranda) in the interior. One other gave access between central Cappadocia and eastern Cilicia.

While the mountains might and did constitute hindrances to communication and transportation, they provided sources of mineral wealth. Since Asia Minor is significant in the biblical narrative during Roman times, only a statement of minerals known and mined then is provided here. The gold of Asia Minor was depleted by Roman times. A little silver was still mined in Pontus and some in central Cappadocia. Some copper was produced at Chalcedon and in Pontus and Cilicia. How many of the abandoned copper pits all over the country were worked in Roman times is not known. Iron came chiefly from Pontus, Cappadocia, Bithynia, and some from the Troad and possibly Caria. Lead was mined in western Mysia. Zinc seems to have been produced in the Troad and on Mount Tmolus. Although various marbles of local importance were quarried, the variegated marble of Docimium was widely exported, as was the white marble of the territory of Cyzicus (modern Kapidagi). The mountains were also important for their timber resources. Forests of pine, oak, and fir abounded in the mountains of both the north and the south.

The Black Sea Coastlands

The Black Sea coast is generally steep and rocky; an irregular line of highlands rises 6,000 to 7,000 feet within 15 to 20 miles from the sea. For the most part there is hardly any intervening coastal plain. Rivers of the region generally are short torrents, which do not provide access to the interior. Moreover, there are few acceptable harbors. All of these drawbacks, plus the risk of earthquakes, tended to hold back the progress of the area.

The northern seaboard of Asia Minor may be divided into two sections. The eastern section consists of the biblical Pontus and Paphlagonia. A persistent northerly wind keeps the area cool and moderately rainy throughout the entire year. But Trapezus (modern Trabzon or Trebizond), the capital of ancient Pontus, enjoys the weather of a Mediterranean Riviera, screened as it is by the Caucasus Range. The mountains are well clad with ship and carpenter's timber and are provided with deposits of silver and iron, which probably gave rise in Hittite days to the earliest iron industry of Nearer Asia. The inner side of the mountains opened to fertile valleys, and the broad valley of the Lycus River served as a main artery for the Pontic area. Poor harbors were always a drawback. But Sinope (modern Sinop), at the most northerly point on the Black Sea coastline, did become a great maritime center.

The western section of the northern seaboard of Asia Minor consists of ancient Bithynia and Mysia. Here the climate is similar to that of the eastern region. There is not so much mineral wealth; but the mountains stand farther back from the coast, leaving room for good grain and orchard country.

Western Asia Minor

The western fringe of Asia Minor contributed most to the country's history in Greek and Roman days. Its weather is milder than that of the Greek homeland, and the soil is more fertile. The coastline in highly intricate and broken, with many irregularly shaped islands.

Beginning in the north, the Bosporus is 16 miles long and on the average 1 mile wide, though it narrows in places to less than 700 yards. Both banks rise steeply from the waters. The Sea of Marmara is a natural creel for trapping shoals of fish on their annual migration from the Mediterranean to the Black Sea. The Dardanelles is 25 miles long and increases in width toward the south, from $2/5$ mile in the north to $4\frac{1}{2}$ miles in the south. Because of evaporation in the Mediterranean, a continuous flow of water south from the Black Sea produces a strong current in the Bosporus and Dardenelles. The current is 3 miles an hour at Istanbul.

As one moves farther south along the Aegean coast, he encounters a series of east-west valleys, which, generally speaking, are broad and flat-bottomed and well-furnished with rich alluvial deposits laid by the rivers. But although this deposit makes for very productive valleys when drained and cultivated, it also contributed to the silting up of river mouths and harbors. For instance, the mouth of the Menderes is now several miles west of where it was in Roman times. The site of Miletus, once a focus of naval communication, is entirely cut off from the sea. The harbor of Ephesus is completely filled in. A further disadvantage of this silting is the creation of marshes with their malarial threat.

In biblical times there were four broad river valleys in western Asia Minor: Caicus, Hermus, Cayster, and Maeander. Each provided access to an important hinterland. Pergamum was located in the Caicus. Smyrna, Sardis, and Philadelphia had access to the Hermus. The Cayster flowed north of Ephesus, and that great city of Diana also tapped the trade of the Maeander, as did Laodicea. In Roman times Miletus also lay on the Maeander.

The towns of western Asia Minor got material for their textile industries from the sheep downs of the Phrygian tableland. Laodicea was known for its black wool, and Pergamum for its brocades and sheep hides made into parchment, which displaced papyrus as a writing material.

The accidents of geography led to the development of two largely distinct cultures in Asia Minor. The culture of the plateau in the interior was essentially oriental, while that of the coastal cities was largely Greek or Greco-Roman.

The Mediterranean Coastlands

Along the entire length of the southern seaboard of Asia Minor, the mountains descend steeply to the sea, except in the regions of Pamphylia and eastern Cilicia. Thus the Mediterranean coastlands entered little into ancient history. The southerly winds of the winter season brought sufficient rainfall for a rich forest growth, which the Egyptians and many after them coveted for timber resources. Western Cilicia was the most trackless part of the coast and served as a pirate hideout.

The mountains of southern Asia Minor are fold ranges, not rift valleys. In the north, the western Taurus folds are so closely packed against the plateau of Anatolia that hardly any streams cut their way through the mountains to the sea. Here the mountains are a serious barrier to contact with the interior, and roads are few. The main Taurus, reaching 12,000 feet, are much higher than the western Taurus. However, they are not as wide as the western Taurus, and erosion is more active. So a number of narrow and steep river valleys have been cut through the mountain chain at several points. One of these gorges is cut by the Yeziloluk, a tributary of the Cydnus, and forms the famous Cilician Gates.

Eastern Asia Minor

Eastern Asia Minor consists of a series of mountain ranges in the north, falling away into broken plateaus and finally into an undulating plain that continues into northern Syria and Iraq.

Climate

The climate of Asia Minor is one of extremes. Parts of the Aegean coastlands never experience frost. In the east snow lies even in the valleys for a third of the year. The Black Sea coastlands have a rainfall that ranges from 25 inches in the west to 100 inches in the east, and a mean temperature of 45° F. for January and 70° for August. The Aegean coastlands have rainfall of 25 to 30 inches and a mean temperature of 45° for January and 75° in July and August. The Mediterranean coastlands have a rainfall of about 30 inches and a mean temperature of 50° in January and 83° in the summer. The central plateau has about 10 to 17 inches of rainfall; all districts have more than 100 days of frost during the year. The January temperature mean is 30°, and the summer mean about 70°. In the east the climate is one of the most difficult and inhospitable in the world, with hot and dry summers and bitterly cold winters. Rainfall averages 17 to 24 inches, and temperatures of 40° below zero have been recorded in January.

Rivers and Lakes

Several rivers already have been mentioned. Others should be noted. The most important river of the peninsula is the Kizil Irmak (ancient Halys), 600 miles long, which originates in eastern Asia Minor and flows in a great bend to the southwest and finally into the Black Sea through what was Pontus. Unfortunately its gorge is often too narrow to permit it to be an important means of communication into the interior. The Sakarya (ancient Sangarius), 300 miles long, originates in what was ancient Phrygia and makes a great bend to the east and flows into the Black Sea through biblical Bithynia. The Cestrus (Köprü, about 80 miles long) was the chief river of Pamphylia. The Calycadnus (about 150 miles long) drained western Cilicia. And the Cydnus (about 40 miles long), the Sarus (780 miles long), and the Pyramus (230 miles long) flowed through eastern Cilicia, the latter two originating in the mountains of Cappadocia.

Numerous lakes might be mentioned. The greatest is Tatta (Tuz), a salt lake in the central plain, some 60 by 10 to 30 miles in winter and a mere marsh in the summer drought. A fine freshwater lake is Karalis (Beysehir), southeast of Pisidian Antioch on the road to Lystra. It is about 35 miles long and lies at 3,770 feet in altitude. Southwest of Pisidian Antioch is Limnai (Egridir), 30 miles long, at 2,850 feet in altitude.

Roads

Numerous roads spanned Asia Minor by the days of Paul and John. The great eastern trade route to the Euphrates began at Ephesus and traversed the Maeander Valley, passing through Laodicea, Colossae, Apamea, then arching north of Pisidian Antioch, dropping south to Galatian Laodicea and cutting east through Cappadocia.

The trade route from Ephesus to Syria would have been the same as the former to Apamea and then would have passed through Pisidian Antioch and Iconium, then south through Laranda or southeast through Hyde, and finally through the Cilician Gates to Tarsus. A fine western road led north from Ephesus through Smyrna, Pergamum, and Adramyttium to Cyzicus. A northern road led east from Byzantium through Nicomedia and Claudiopolis in Bithynia and then arched northward through Pompeiopolis and dipped south to Amisia. Other lesser north-south and east-west routes could be noted.

Paul's Birthplace

Although it is impossible to comment in detail on the geographical situation of all the biblical towns of Asia Minor, certain ones hold special interest for the student: Paul's birthplace, the cities of the first missionary journey, Ephesus—Paul's long-term place of ministry on the third missionary journey, the towns of the Lycus Valley, and the seven cities of the Revelation.

After the howling mob had brought about Paul's arrest in Jerusalem, he tried to establish himself with the Roman chiliarch (an officer in charge of one thousand men) with the assertion "I am . . . a Jew of Tarsus in Cilicia, a citizen of no mean city" (Acts 21:39). The allegation won him the respect of the chiliarch and the right to address his attackers; Tarsus was one of the great cities of Asia Minor during the first century A.D. But Tarsus was a city in Cilicia; and in order to gain proper understanding of the city, it is necessary first to consider its environs.

Cilicia. Geographically, Cilicia referred to the area of southeastern Asia Minor between Pamphylia on the west, the Amanus Mountains on the east, Lycaonia and Cappadocia on the north, and the Mediterranean on the south. It had a coastline of about 430 miles, extending from the eastern boundary of Pamphylia to the southern end of the Gulf of Issus. Politically (in Paul's day at least) Cilicia designated the Roman province that encompassed the eastern part of the geographical area. When Luke spoke of the "sea of Cilicia" (Acts 27:5), he probably had in mind the Mediterranean opposite the entire geographical region. Since Paul used Roman political terminology, he must have applied Cilicia to the Roman province only (e.g., Acts 21:39; 22:3).

Cilicia was commonly divided into two territories, as dissimilar in their physical characteristics as they could be. The western part, Cilicia Tracheia, was a tangled mass of mountains descending abruptly to the sea, with a narrow tract of land along the coast and little or no plain country. The eastern part of Cilicia was known as Cilicia Pedias. Roughly speaking, this area was triangular in shape, its apex at the northeast formed by the Amanus and Taurus Mountains. The former ran due south and separated Cilicia from Syria; the latter ran southwest to the sea, cutting off the region from Cappadocia and Lycaonia. The third side of the triangle was the Mediterranean. Three rivers watered Pedias and flowed in a southwesterly direction. On each river a city developed. On the westernmost, the Cydnus, rose the great city of Tarsus. The lower valley of these rivers now contains about 800 square miles of arable land, with a strip of dunes and lagoons some 2 to 3 miles wide stretching along the coast.

Cilicia Pedias had much in its favor from a geographical standpoint. Its land was fertile and grew cereals of all kinds, and its flax made possible a thriving linen industry. Timber from the nearby mountains moved through Cilician ports. Goats living on the slopes of the Taurus, where snow lies until May, grew magnificent coats used in the famous tentmaking industry of the area. This is the trade that Paul followed (Acts 18:3). The fact that Pedias was located on one of the great trade routes of the ancient world, the most frequented land route from the East to the Aegean, promoted commerce and industry and contributed to the growth of towns. The trade route coming from the Euphrates over the Amanus Pass and another trade route coming from Antioch in Syria via the Syrian Gates met about 50 miles east of Tarsus, entered the city as a single road, swung north through the Cilician Gates, and led across south central Asia Minor to Ephesus.

About 30 miles north of Tarsus were the Cilician Gates, a narrow gorge that originally was just wide enough to allow passage of the small stream that ran through it. With much effort the Tarsians in early times widened the gorge and built a wagon road up to its approaches and through it. Their industry put them in possession of the one wagon road across the Taurus Mountains.

Tarsus. Tarsus was located about 10 miles from the Mediterranean at 80 feet above sea level. Normally the oppressive atmosphere of such a place would have been most destructive of vigorous municipal or commercial life. But about 2 miles north of the city the hills began to rise gently and extended in undulating ridges until they met the Taurus. And about 10 miles north of the lowland city, a second Tarsus rose. Partly a summer residence, it served a considerable population as a year-round home. The more bracing climate of the upland town provided a means of offsetting the enervating climate of the lower region.

In New Testament times Tarsus lay astride the Cydnus River, which was then navigable by light vessels right into the middle of the city. However, most ships docked at the harbor, which was 5 to 6 miles south of the city. At that point was a spring-fed lake, Rhegma, around all but the south sides of which extended the harbor town and wharf installations. Great skill and diligence must have been expended on maintaining the channel of the Cydnus and the harbor. In later centuries, slackness required an auxiliary channel to reduce flooding. The cut to the east of town (made by Justinian, A.D. 537-63) in time became the main bed of the river and remains so today. Ramsay thinks the population of the three parts of Tarsus (city proper, hill town, and harbor) reached a half million.[1]

Cities of the First Missionary Journey

On his first missionary journey Paul sailed from Cyprus to Perga on the Asia Minor coast and almost immediately traveled inland to evangelize. His first major stop, Antioch of Pisidia, stood about 100 miles north of Perga and was one of a chain of military colonies founded by Augustus to control the wild tribes of Pisidia and Pamphylia. It was the administrative center of the southern half of the province of Galatia.

About 80 miles to the southeast was Iconium (modern Konya), at

1. Sir William Ramsay, *The Cities of St. Paul* (London: Hodder & Stoughton, n.d.), p. 97.

the edge of the central plateau of Asia Minor. Iconium stood on a level plateau about 3,400 feet above sea level. Although Iconium was unsuited for defense, a site such as this with an everflowing natural supply of water and fertile soil was a center of human life among arid plateaus. During the first century, it controlled the fertile district around it for some 200 square miles.

About 18 miles southwest of Iconium stood Lystra, founded as a Roman colony by Augustus, probably in 6 B.C., for the purpose of training and regulating the mountain tribes on the southern frontier of the province of Galatia. It seems to have been a place of some importance under the early emperors. The city stood on a small, elongated hill in the center of a valley abundantly supplied with water by two streams. Lystra possessed a considerable territory of fertile soil in the valley, as well as a tract of low hilly ground. Derbe, though traditionally identified with Gudelisin, has in the last few years been almost certainly shown by inscriptions to have been located at the village of Kerti Hüyük, some 40 miles east of Iconium (Konya).

The account of Paul's travels in Asia Minor on his first missionary journey appears in Acts 13:13—14:25. On his second missionary journey he returned to visit the churches founded earlier (Acts 16:1-6).

Ephesus

During Paul's third missionary journey the focus of attention centered on Ephesus, largest city of Asia (the Roman province that occupied about the western third of Asia Minor). The population of this city, at least late in the century when John lived there, probably reached a half million. Paul evangelized there for at least two years and three months (Acts 19:8, 10).

Ephesus stood at the entrance to one of the four clefts in the hills of west central Asia Minor. It was along these valleys that the roads across the central plateau of Asia Minor passed. (Other great cities standing at the entrance to passes into the interior were Pergamum, Smyrna, and Miletus.) Chief of these four routes ran up the Maeander and Lycus valleys to Apamea and eastward. Miletus and Ephesus both contested for mastery of the trade flowing over this route. The latter won out because the track across the hills from the main road to Ephesus was shorter than the road to Miletus and because the pass to

Miletus was at a considerably higher altitude. As already noted, Ephesus was also on the great north-south road of western Asia Minor and was on the main sea route from Rome to the east. Its importance came also from its political prominence as the seat of the Roman governor of the province of Asia and as the location of the great temple of Diana — rated as one of the seven wonders of the ancient world.

Ephesus was approximately 4 miles from the sea, but its inland harbor was connected with the Cayster River, which wound through the plain to the north of the city. The harbor was kept large enough and deep enough only by constant dredging; and when the empire declined and efforts to maintain the harbor slackened, it silted up entirely.

Towns of the Lycus Valley

Three towns of the Lycus Valley figure in the New Testament narrative: Colossae, Hierapolis, and Laodicea (Colossians 2:1; 4:13-16; Revelation 3:14-22). The last is important as one of the seven cities John addressed in the Revelation. Colossae is more prominent in the New Testament because it has a whole epistle addressed to it; but believers at Laodicea were also encouraged to read that letter (Colossians 4:16).

The best way to introduce these Lycus cities to the modern student is to take him on a journey up the Maeander River from its mouth near Miletus. As one travels inland, the broad and fertile Maeander Valley becomes narrower; and about 75 miles from its mouth the foothills compress the valley to a width of about a mile. Approximately 25 miles farther on, the Maeander makes a sharp turn northward. At the bend it is joined by the Lycus (which flows northwest), one of its principal tributaries. The traveler is now in the open Lycus Valley.

Roughly triangular in form, the plain of the Lycus (which runs from southeast to northwest) is about 24 miles long. At its widest, the plain is 6 miles. It is hemmed in on all sides by highlands.

About 12 miles southeast of the junction of the Lycus with the Maeander stood ancient Laodicea. This city was situated on the long spur of a hill between the narrow valleys of two small rivers that emptied their waters into the Lycus. Laodicea stood at an altitude of about 850 feet, approximately 3 miles south of the Lycus, some 100 miles from Ephesus. The great road from the coast to the interior passed right through the middle of the city, making it an important center of trade and communication. The city's wealth came from its favorable location on the east-west commercial route across Asia Minor and especially from its production of a very fine quality of world-famous black, glossy wool. It was also a center of banking (Cicero was one of its more famous customers) and had a celebrated school of medicine nearby.

As one strolled out through the north gate of Laodicea, he could see the white cliffs of Hierapolis, 6 miles away, gleaming in the sunshine. The water from the hot springs of the place has tumbled over the cliffs from earliest times, depositing its heavy content of carbonates, sodium, and chlorides of calcium in its wake. Though from a distance the cliff looks blinding white, one can see on closer inspection that it is streaked with yellow and black and gives the appearance of a frozen waterfall. The city was situated on a shelf about 1,100 feet above sea level and 150 to 300 feet above the plain.

Colossae lay near the upper end of the valley, about 11 miles east of Laodicea. At Colossae the valley narrowed to approximately two miles, and the city was overshadowed by great mountain heights. The fortified acropolis of the city lay on the south bank of the Lycus, but buildings and tombs stretched out on the north bank.

The Cities of the Revelation

The seven cities of the Revelation were apparently addressed by John because they already had achieved preeminence among the churches of Asia. All seven stood on the important circular road that brought together the most populous and most prosperous part of the province of Asia. The order in which they lay on the Roman road is precisely the order in which they are addressed in Revelation 2-3. The distances between these cities by road in English miles is as follows: Ephesus to Smyrna, 42; Smyrna to Pergamum, 65; Pergamum to Thyatira, 44; Thyatira to Sardis, 33; Sardis to Philadelphia, 26; Philadelphia to Laodicea, 47; Laodicea to Ephesus, 99.

Something has been said already about Ephesus and Laodicea. Smyrna, modern Izmir, was located in the same spot as the modern city, at the southeast edge of the Gulf of Smyrna. Smyrna was a beautiful city. Located beside the beautiful Aegean Sea, it possessed a good harbor—a double one, in fact. The outer harbor was a portion of the gulf and served as a mooring ground; the inner harbor, now silted in, had a narrow entrance that could be blocked by a chain. The city itself curved around the edge of the bay at the base of 515-foot Mount Pagus, its splendid acropolis.

Pergamum, situated on a hill about 1,000 feet high, commanded the fertile valley of the Caicus River. The city was located about 3 miles north of the Caicus and about 18 miles from the ocean opposite the island of Lesbos. Pergamum communicated with the sea via the Caicus, which was navigable for small native craft. From the city a highway ran to the interior of Asia Minor almost to the border of the province of Asia. It was also located on the important north-south road which ran from Ephesus to Cyzicus. While the city was the capital of the kingdom of Pergamum, it was located on its magnificent acropolis. During the Roman period there was also a lower city of considerable extent that spread around the foot of the acropolis.

Thyatira stood on the bank of a stream that poured its waters into the Hermus River. It stood at about 330 feet in altitude, commanded a fertile plain, and was located on a main commercial route. Thyatira apparently had more trade guilds than any other Asian city. It will be remembered that Lydia, a seller of purple from Thyatira, probably represented her guild at Philippi (Acts 16:14). In addition to its commercial importance, Thyatira was a station on the imperial post road that extended from Rome, across Greece, Asia Minor, and Syria, all the way to Alexandria in Egypt.

Sardis dominated the region of the Hermus River and its tributaries, the broadest and most fertile of all the river basins of Asia Minor. She commanded the great trade and military road from the Aegean islands into the interior of the peninsula. On a 1,000-foot-high acropolis about 5 miles south of the Hermus stood early Sardis. The site forms a small, elongated plateau with steep sides, so that the ancient city was virtually impregnable. While Sardis was capital of the kingdom of Lydia, it was largely confined to its acropolis. But during the Roman period it spread extensively over the valley below.

Philadelphia (about 100 miles from Smyrna) was located at about 800 feet in altitude on a broad hill that slopes up gently from the valley toward the Tmolus Mountains. Northeast of the city lay a great vine-growing district, which contributed greatly to its prosperity. It was a center for pacification and acculturation of the central regions of the Pergamene kingdom and was, like Thyatira, an important stop on the imperial post road that extended around the eastern Mediterranean.

The great cities of Asia have received considerable attention at the hands of archaeologists during the last century. One may again walk down the streets of Ephesus of the days of Paul and John. He may climb over the acropolis of Pergamum and see ruins of its ancient glories. He may observe Sardis coming to life as a result of extensive excavation there in recent years. Although much is yet to be done, enough has been accomplished to help the modern student appreciate more fully the truth that Asia Minor is a Bible land.

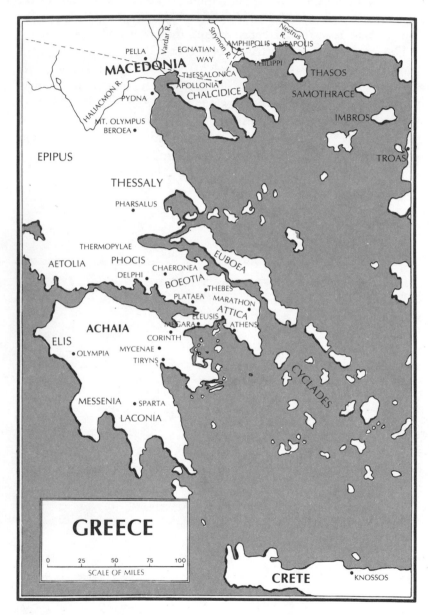

GREECE

0	25	50	75	100

SCALE OF MILES

9

Greece

Greece has special significance in the biblical narrative in connection with Paul's second missionary journey. Here he launched missions in Europe at the prayer meeting by the riverside at Philippi. Here he preached at Thessalonica, Berea, Athens, and especially at Corinth, where he remained for eighteen months. To the Greeks the apostle wrote six New Testament books: 1 and 2 Thessalonians, 1 and 2 Corinthians, Philippians, and Titus addressed to Paul's lieutenant while Titus ministered on the island of Crete.

The Boundaries of Greece

The geographical bounds of Greece have been variously placed. In classical times Greece, or Hellas, was the southern projection of the Balkan Peninsula, stretching south from Thessaly and Epirus, and including the Ionian and Aegean islands. Covering approximately 30,000 square miles, this Greece was about the size of Scotland or Maine.

Subsequently, as Macedonia was Hellenized, it came to be considered part of the Greek world. Those who include Macedonia as part of Greece have in mind an area covering some 50,000 square miles, comparable to that of England or Alabama. Probably Crete also should be included as part of the Greek world, raising the total by 3,200 square miles, thus constituting an area about the size of Florida or Wisconsin. Modern Greece comprises much of ancient Macedonia and Thrace, the Greek peninsula, Crete, and the islands of the Aegean — about 51,000 square miles.

The Hellas of the days of the apostle Paul (when the biblical narrative becomes most involved with the area) was very differently constituted. Crete was a Roman province by itself. The coast of Asia Minor and the adjacent islands comprised part of the province of Asia. The province of Thrace occupied eastern Greece. Macedonia and northern Greece were incorporated into the province of Macedonia. The rest of the peninsula and a number of Aegean islands formed the province of Achaea. At one point Luke described the last two of the above-mentioned provinces as Macedonia and Greece (Acts 20:1-2).

The Mountains

Dominant in the life of any Greek were the mountains and the sea. Mountains covered two-thirds to three-fourths of the land surface, leaving not more than 25 percent of cultivable soil. No other country of the Mediterranean area presents a more tumbled surface than Greece; so while the mountains of Greece are not especially high, they are seldom out of sight.

Mount Olympus, the highest of the Greek mountains (located in the northeastern corner of the peninsula), is only about 9,600 feet; and few of the others are over 8,000 feet. Those that are include Mount Pindus (8,130 feet), Mount Ida in Crete (8,060 feet), and Mount Parnassus (8,060 feet). Thus, the capacity of Greek mountains for holding snow is limited, and the regularity of water supply is affected.

Although the placement of mountains in Greece is chaotic, there is a degree of symmetry. The Magnesian Range extends south from Olympus in eastern Greece; the Pindus Range lies between Thessaly and Epirus in central Greece; and the Epirus Range stretches along the western coast. These are crossed by other ridges, dividing the country into a vast checkerboard of tiny valleys, few of which are more than 12 miles long and more than half as wide. Often the mountain passes between these valleys are 3,000 feet or more in altitude and buried in snow at least part of the winter. With communications so hampered, a provincialism developed in Greece such as has probably existed in no other historically important area of the world. Moreover, it was the mountain barriers that contributed much to the city-state development of ancient Greece. Though periodic efforts were made to overcome this suicidal division, none was really successful until Macedonia, Rome, and other powers exerted an external pressure for unity.

In ancient times language, religion, the great athletic games and festivals, and the influence of the Homeric epics were among features that contributed to a bond of union among the Greeks or at least helped them to feel they were different from other people.

Rivers

Down from the mountainsides coursed the rivers of Greece. They were mostly unnavigable winter and spring torrents that flooded the arable land, and washed soil away from the hillsides during the rainy season. During the dry season some of them formed stagnant pools, while those with dry beds served as highways for travelers. The rivers were mainly a hindrance to Greece, eroding the land, forming breeding places for malarial mosquitoes, silting the mouths of rivers so their harbors were virtually useless, and impeding travel. During floods these rivers were difficult to cross for both man and animal. Bridges were almost an impossibility for streams that varied from a few feet in width to more than 500 feet with the seasons. Moreover, these streams were too muddy to serve as a water supply for men or animals. The larger rivers of Greece proper were the Peneus (Salambria) in Thessaly (about 125 miles long), the Achelous in western Greece (100 miles long), the Arachthus (Arakhthos) in Epirus (80 miles long); and the Alpheus in the western Peloponnesus (75 miles long); but some of the smaller ones were more prominent in song and story. Rivers of Macedonia are noted later.

The Sea

Although the mountains dominated the landscape of Greece and also affected her politics, economy, and climate, the sea was also a major factor in Greek life. While the mountains almost closed Greece to the European continent, she was accessible on her seafronts. The coast is so deeply indented that Greece has the longest coastline in proportion to enclosed area of all important historical regions. With a coast of 2,600 miles, it exceeds Italy's (2,150 miles) and that of the Iberian Peninsula (2,300), though its land area is only one-third of the former and one-sixth of the latter. As a result, nowhere in central or southern Greece will a person be more than 40 miles from the sea.

The many indentations afforded numerous harbors. When men sailed the Aegean, they were never out of sight of land on a clear day, until they moved south of Crete into the eastern Mediterranean. Navigation in the Aegean was almost reduced to the simplicity of a ferry service.

So the Greeks, unable to wrest a living from the rocky farms, became a seafaring people. Learning from all the peoples with whom they came in contact, they cross-fertilized the whole Mediterranean area. It is significant for the history of Hellas that her best ports and many of her valleys lay on the east coast. Therefore, her eastern areas received civilizing influences from the Orient first. In contrast, Italy faced west and was slowed in receiving eastern culture.

It is easy, however, to overemphasize the place of the sea in Greek economic life. The mountains adjacent to many of the city-states did not produce good ship timber and sometimes were literally a barrier between the inhabitants and the sea. Moreover, the Aegean waters are too clear and devoid of plant life to support large schools of fish. And overseas trade was not vital in the early days when most of the communities of Greece were self-sufficient.

Then, too, the seas around Greece are typically Mediterranean. In winter the Adriatic Sea is a storm center; gusty north winds plague the northern Aegean. The surrounding seas remained closed to all Greeks in winter and to some Greeks most of the time. Sheer cliffs line a good part of the Greek coast. The Thessalians and Boeotians always remained landsmen. The inhabitants of Corinth and Megara were the only peoples of the Peloponnesus or of the area around the Corinthian Gulf to have much of an overseas trade. Sparta broke out of her landlocked condition for a period only during and after her great war with Athens (431-404 B.C.), when she built a navy with the help of Persia. Even the peoples of the Aegean Islands were not seafarers continually.

It should be remembered that the Greeks have always been primarily rural and agricultural. As late as the end of the nineteenth century,

70 percent of them still lived in rural areas. The lack of soil forced them to terrace the hillsides and plant grapevines, olive trees, and whatever else they could produce on some very unpromising land. The stony nature of the soil often forced them to raise barley and millet rather than wheat. Pasturelands were more suited to the raising of sheep and goats than cattle. Most of their wheat was imported.

Climate

The climate of Greece is mild and has not changed appreciably in at least the last 2,000 years. Northern Greece has a climate similar to that of the Continent with a fair amount of snow, whereas southern Greece has a climate more Mediterranean in nature. Cold winds, however, bring snow even to Athens in winter. There are two seasons: rainy, or winter (October to April); and dry, or summer (May to September). The winters are rather boisterous, but not devoid of sunshine. Rainfall is fairly heavy, measuring 40 inches in the west and slightly less in the east. In summers there is little precipitation. This period of drought lasts for two months in the north and four months in the Peloponnesus. The hot summer sun is tempered by sea breezes in most places, but some of the cup-shaped valleys are effectively isolated from this relief by the surrounding mountains. In such places summer weather is equal to that of the tropics. For instance, at Larissa in the Thessalian Basin July has a mean temperature of 90°.

Natural Resources

"To Hellas poverty has always been a foster sister,"[1] Herodotus well observed. It is certainly remarkable that this minor poverty-stricken people was able to soar above its environmental limitations and produce great cultural achievements. Something already has been said about the poor quality and small amount of arable soil in Greece. Whereas in most ancient times there was a considerable amount of timber, by the fifth century B.C. Greece was no longer able to supply her needs and had to import.

---

1. Ancient Greece presented a greater impression of prosperity than some of the terrain today. Hillsides terraced and, covered with a mantle of trees, were less subject to erosion than they have been since. Many rocky slopes in Greece had a thin topsoil on them.

Neither did she have much in the way of minerals. Silver and lead were mined in Attica, iron and copper in Euboea and Laconia, and gold east of Philippi and on the islands of Siphnos and Thasos. Most of the ancient minefields are now exhausted. Some fields that do exist were never exploited in antiquity. There were considerable supplies of potters' clay, especially at Athens and Corinth. Greece had plenty of good building stone and was famous for her marble.

The finest of the white marbles were quarried in the Cyclades (islands in the south Aegean) and on Mount Pentelicus in Attica. Although Pentelic marble had a smooth grain, the ancient Greeks preferred the marble of Paros, which was more translucent, for sculpture. The only colored marbles of Greece quarried extensively in ancient times were the white and green *cipollino* of Euboea, much desired by the Roman emperors, and the *verde antico* (old green) of northern Thessaly.

Areas of Greece Significant for Bible Study

Macedonia. At the north of Hellas lay Macedonia. Since its boundaries varied over the centuries and since the exact boundaries during much of the country's history are not known, it is hard indeed to describe its exact size. The kingdom was, however, always located at the northeast corner of the Aegean; and Pella (24 miles northwest of Thessalonica) was the capital during much of its history. Under Philip II (359-336 B.C.), Macedonia came to include Thrace and to dominate all of Greece. Under Alexander the Great it conquered the entire Persian Empire.

When Macedonia became a Roman province in 148 B.C., and throughout most of the first century A.D., the boundaries of the territory were quite well fixed. The Macedonia in which Paul ministered had a borderline that stretched from a point near the Nestos River in eastern Greece to the Adriatic at approximately the latitude of Tiranë (Tirana), modern capital of Albania, then south to the northern border of Epirus, which it skirted to its southern end, and then eastward to the Gulf of Volos (ancient Pagasaeus). Therefore it may be seen that the province included not only most of the northern part of modern

Greece, but also portions of Bulgaria and Yugoslavia and about half of Albania.

Although Macedonia was very mountainous, it also had some fertile plains along the northern rim of the Aegean. Four great rivers—west to east, the Haliacmon (Vistritsa), Anios (Vardar), Strymon, and Nestos—of the European type (which flow all year instead of drying up in the summer) break through the coastal ridges to the sea and deposit around their mouths rich alluvial plains. In the west, the Haliacmon and Vardar plains have been joined at least since the fifth century B.C. Moving east, one comes to the Strymonic Plain, which is the most fertile plain of the north Aegean area. Next comes the Philippian Plain, and finally, the Nestos Plain.

When the apostle Paul came to Greece, he landed first in Macedonia at the port of Neapolis. Almost immediately he journeyed 13 miles inland to Philippi, which had been founded by Philip of Macedon and was in pre-Roman days the chief mining center of the Pangaeus gold fields. These mines seem to have been worked out by New Testament times.[2] Philippi spread out in the plain to the south of its acropolis, which towered over the city to a height of more than 1,000 feet.

After successful ministry in Philippi, accompanied by suffering for the gospel (Acts 16), Paul traveled westward through Macedonia on the Egnatian Way (main highway across Greece) through Amphipolis (about 35 miles from Philippi) and Apollonia (approximately 25 miles farther west) and finally came to Thessalonica (about 40 miles west of Apollonia). This city rose at the edge of the Gulf of Thessalonica in amphitheater form on the slopes of the foothills of the Cortiates Mountains. In New Testament times it was significant as the capital of the province of Macedonia and as a great center for trade by land and sea. Its population was perhaps 200,000. Here, as at Philippi, the apostle had a successful ministry accompanied by opposition and suffering.

Attica. From Macedonia Paul traveled to Athens on the peninsula of Attica, an important area of eastern Greece. Though very significant for the history of civilization, this small territory comprises only about 1,000 square miles and is approximately the size of Rhode Island. The peninsula is roughly triangular in shape and measures some 40 miles east and west and a like distance north and south. No spot in Attica is

2. The Greek government has been trying to reactivate these gold fields, but so far they have had little success.

more than 25 miles in a straight line from Athens.

Those who are enamored with the greatness of this area often are unaware of its drawbacks. It is the driest region of Greece, with an average annual rainfall of only 16 inches. Only about one-fourth of its soil is arable, and part of that will raise nothing but olives. On the credit side of the ledger are a coast where the mountains leave room for easy landing places, excellent clay beds for pottery manufacture, the famous marble of Mount Pentelicus, and the lead and silver mines of Laurium in the south of the peninsula (largely exhausted by the time of the Christian Era).

Athens was the center of all of life in Attica. In the middle of Athens stood the acropolis, her citadel in early days and location of incomparable temples in classical and New Testament times. This isolated hill about 5 miles from the coast, rises to a height of 512 feet, about 300 to 400 feet above the town. It has an almost vertical drop on all sides but the west. Adjacent to the acropolis on the northwest stands the Areopagus or Mars Hill, at an altitude of 377 feet (see Acts 17). To the east of the acropolis Lycabettus thrusts its sharply pointed top above pine-clad slopes to a height of 1,112 feet. South of Athens stretches the Hymettus Range (3,370 feet high). In the evening its barren western flank is colored a flaming purple by the reflected rays of the setting sun. Apparently this beautiful sight led the ancient poet Pindar to describe Athens as the "violet-crowned city." After about 500 B.C. the great port of Athens was developed at Piraeus. Another important town of Attica was Eleusis, a religious center 14 miles northwest of Athens.

The Peloponnesus, including Corinth. As Paul moved southwest of Athens, he crossed the Isthmus of Corinth and entered the Peloponnesus. This peninsula, shaped like a mulberry leaf, has actually been an island since the Corinth Canal was finished in A.D. 1893. Slightly smaller than New Hampshire, the Peloponnesus had several important districts; the most important of these in New Testament times was Corinth. The Peloponnesus formed the larger part of the Roman province of Achaea, organized in 27 B.C.

Occupying the northeast corner of the Peloponnesus was the city-state of Corinth, which controlled a territory about one-fourth that of Attica. Blessed with considerable deposits of white and cream-colored clay, Corinth developed the most prolific ceramic industry of early

Greece, but after about 550-525 B.C. it lost out to Athenian competition in the field.

More important to the development of Corinth, however, was her geographical position. Located a mile and a half south of the Isthmus of Corinth, she commanded this 4-mile-wide neck of land, as well as its eastern port of Cenchrea (Acts 18:18) and its western port of Lechaeum. In New Testament as well as classical times, a large amount of shipping passed through Greek waters, and the trip around the southern tip of Greece was not only long but extremely dangerous. Therefore it became customary to transport goods across the Isthmus of Corinth, saving more than 150 miles. Smaller ships were pulled across the Isthmus on a tramway; larger ones were unloaded and their cargoes reloaded on the other side. Corinth sponsored the Isthmian Games (in honor of Poseidon—god of the sea) at the festival center at the Isthmus every two years (1 Corinthians 9:24-27). The Acropolis of Corinth towered about 1,500 feet over the city to an altitude of 1,886 feet. The city and its acropolis were enclosed by a wall over 6 miles in circumference. Corinth served as the capital of the Roman province of Achaea.

Crete. Crete is the southernmost and largest of the Greek islands. It is the fourth largest island in the Mediterranean (Sicily, Sardinia, and Cyprus being larger). Located 60 miles south of Cape Malea in the Peloponnesus and 110 miles west of Cape Krio in Asia Minor (with Rhodes and other islands between it and Cape Krio), its location made inevitable its use as a seedbed and distributing center for the cultures of the Near East from the fourth to the first millennia B.C.

Composed of an area of 3,200 square miles (about half the size of New Jersey), Crete is of elongated form—160 miles from east to west and 6 to 35 miles from north to south. While the northern coast is deeply indented and provides a good natural harbor at least at Suda at the western end of the island, the southern coast is less indented. In the southern part of the island, the mountains often appear to rise from the sea.

In the center of the southern coast is Cape Lithinos, the southernmost point of the island. Immediately to the east of that is the small bay of Kali Limenes, or Fair Havens, where the ship carrying Paul to Rome took refuge (Acts 27:8). A little less than 25 miles southwest of Cape Lithinos lies the rocky, treeless isle of Clauda (modern Gavdos), which Paul's ship passed as it began to fight the storm that eventually blew it to Malta (Acts 27:16). Crete was a separate Roman province when Paul passed it and when Titus ministered there, having been conquered by Rome 68-67 B.C.

Although mountains cover much of Crete, there are plains, the largest of which is the Messara Plain (in the center of the island), extending about 37 miles in length and 10 miles in breadth. One of the richest plains in Greece, it no doubt supplied the wine and olive oil for the huge storage jars found in the palaces at Knossos (Cnossus) and Phaistos (Phaestus), the chief cities in the north and south of Crete respectively in the days of Minoan greatness. Probably the Messara also furnished orchard produce, which served as a chief staple in the early trade of Cretan merchants. Crete is commonly identified with Caphtor, original home of the Philistines (Amos 9:7).

Although Greece was geographically at a disadvantage in competition with some of the better land of the Mediterranean region, and although she had suffered greatly under the military and political domination of Rome, she was still populous and proud and economically resurgent in the middle of the first century A.D. Moreover, she was responsive to the gospel. Here Paul established the first beachhead of Christianity in Europe.

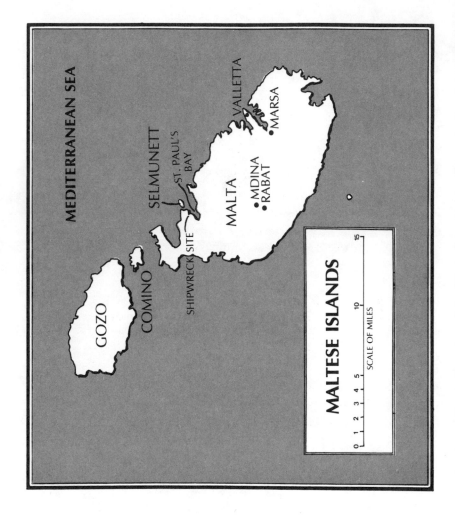

MEDITERRANEAN SEA

GOZO

COMINO

SELMUNETT

ST. PAUL'S BAY

SHIPWRECK SITE

MALTA

MDINA
RABAT

VALLETTA

MARSA

MALTESE ISLANDS

0 1 2 3 4 5   10   15
SCALE OF MILES

10

Malta

The sovereign[1] state of Malta is just as much a Bible land as any of the other territories discussed in this book. Though the number of Bible verses devoted to Malta is small (Acts 28:1-11), the apostle Paul spent three months there after being shipwrecked while on the way to Rome (Acts 12:11); and as a result of his ministry, interest in the gospel apparently was great. The governor, Publius, was very kind to the apostle and the others on board the lost vessel. Tradition has it that he was converted, became the first bishop of Malta, and was later martyred in Athens. According to the Acts narrative, Publius's father was healed in answer to the apostle's prayers, and numerous other individuals experienced healing at the same time.

Although some have claimed in the past that an island in the Adriatic Sea was where the apostle really landed, it now seems beyond all reasonable doubt that the African Melita (Malta) is the correct identification. The Romans called the island Melita and gave the same name to the principal town. The Arabs called the town Mdina, and for centuries it was the only place of any size on the island.

Paul landed on Malta in A.D. 60, according to numerous popular and more scholarly works on Malta. The date may be correct and certainly fits some of the better chronologies of Paul's life, but it is impossible to

---

1. Independent September 21, 1964.

be dogmatic on the point. The islanders still celebrate February 10 as St. Paul's Shipwreck Day, but the date seems highly unlikely. The season closed to shipping in the Mediterranean in ancient times ran from about November 10 to March 10. The Acts passage specifically states that the 276 stranded travelers on their way to Rome spent three months on Malta, and the implication is that as early as possible in the spring they boarded a ship that had wintered in Malta and sailed for Italy. If they sailed before the end of March, then they must have arrived in early January or late December.

Malta is an arid, rocky islet 58 miles south of Sicily, 149 miles south of the European mainland, and 180 miles north of Cape Bon in Tunisia. A little over 17 miles long and 9 miles wide, with a shoreline of 85 miles, it is the chief island of the Maltese group—which also includes Gozo and Comino Islands. The island of Malta with its 95 square miles of land is of limestone formation with thin but fertile soil. Actually, the rocks that make up the islands are basically in the form of a sand-wich—hard limestone on top and bottom with softer rocks between. The softer Globigerina limestone (the filling in the sandwich) is easily quarried and provides the main building stone used on the islands. It hardens with exposure to atmosphere.

Malta consists of a low plateau that descends by gentle steps to the low plain in the southeastern part of the island. There are no high mountains; the Bingemna hills rise to an altitude of 726 feet. Sheer cliffs rise on the southwest coast to a height of 400 feet or more. The coastline is well-indented—especially on the east, northeast, and south-east sides—and provides deep and safe harbors.

Malta is without significant natural resources. But it has often been important for its strategic location as a base from which to control the Mediterranean narrows. Moreover, it is big enough to hold a large garrison and has an excellent harbor—large and deep enough to accom-modate a considerable fleet.

Agriculture has been the chief occupation of Malta for much of its history, but uncertain rainfall makes farming a rather risky business. With an average rainfall of 20 to 22 inches per year, Malta actually has a rainfall that varies from 10 to 40 inches; some periods of drought have extended over three years. There are no rivers or rivulets on the island. Springs flow, but the largest part of the water supply is pumped from strata just above sea level. The climate is temperate and healthful for the greater part of the year, with a mean annual temperature of 64.5° F. The high of 92° is reached in July, and a minimum of 46° is reached in January.

Paul and Malta

The traditional site of Paul's shipwreck is 8 miles northwest of the present capital of Valletta at a place now called St. Paul's Bay. Careful students have pointed out that the traditional site fits all the intimations of the biblical narrative. As the sailors on board Paul's Alexandrian ship came to the entrance to the bay, they thought they were nearing land; they could see the breakers but not the low-lying land. Then they took two soundings of 20 and 15 fathoms, confirming their belief. They apparently decided to run the ship aground, but feared to do it in the dark because they might dash the ship to pieces on the rocks and all might perish. So they cast four anchors from the stern and waited for daybreak. At dawn, after having eaten their first good meal in two weeks, they hoisted sail, cut their anchors, and made for the sandy beach at the end of the bay. As they made for shore, the bow of the ship stuck fast in "a place where two seas met," apparently meaning a strait. Luke must have meant the channel between the Selmunett islet, which stretched across the northwest entrance to St. Paul's Bay and the island of Malta. The conclusion is, then, that the ship ran aground at modern Irdum Ilbies, inside St. Paul's Bay, just southwest of the islet of Selmunett. Although the ship broke up under the merciless pounding of the waves, all the passengers and crew reached land safely. A statue of Paul has stood on Selmunett since the middle of the last century.

Publius, the governor, befriended the refugees from the storm. His house has been traditionally located on the spot in Mdina where the Cathedral of St. Peter and St. Paul stands today. And a cave is shown at nearby Rabat, where Paul is supposed to have lived during his three-month stay on the island. Above the grotto stands a chapel today. However, Italian excavations at the site of the church of St. Paul Milqi (St. Paul Welcomed) near St. Paul's Bay have revealed a series of superimposed churches built over a Roman villa. This was a pilgrimage site connected with Paul and may have been the location of Publius's home.

Malta was certainly very prosperous when Paul arrived. Just before the birth of Christ, the historian and geographer Diodorus Siculus wrote of Malta:

> It has many useful harbours; the inhabitants are very rich; artisans of every class are to be found amongst them; the most expert are such as make textiles famous for their firmness and softness. The houses are very beautiful and ambitiously adorned with cornices and stucco work.[2]

In the center of the island, where Mdina and Rabat now stand, was the fortified capital, connected by a road to port facilities and possibly a harborside town in the Marsa area. The countryside was dotted with villas, many of which have been excavated. Agriculture was geared primarily to the production of wheat and olives. Malta produced a number of luxury goods for export. Luke called the inhabitants *barbaroi*, signifying a non-Greco-Roman people (Acts 28:2), which tallies with the testimony of Diodorus Siculus that they were Phoenicians— neither Hellenized nor Romanized—and that they spoke a dialect of Phoenician. A colony of Carthage, Malta had come under Roman control in 218 B.C. The high level of prosperity attained while Carthage ruled continued for several centuries after the Roman conquest.

---

2. F. R. G. Pearce, *Illustrated Guide to Historic Malta*, 4th ed. (Malta: Giov. Muscat, 1967), p. 34.

ALPS MOUNTAINS

Po River

APENNINE

Arno R.

Rubicon R.

ETRURIA

LATIUM

ELBA

Tiber R.

Anio R.

MOUNTAINS

ADRIATIC SEA

CORSICA

VEII

ROME

OSTIA

THREE TAVERNS

APPII FORUM

TUSCAN SEA

PUTEOLI

APPIAN WAY

BRUNDISIUM

CAMPANIA

POMPEII

TARENTUM

SARDINIA

THURII

TARENTUM

GULF

ITALY

0 25 50 100 200

SCALE OF MILES

MEDITERRANEAN

RHEGIUM

MESSANA

IONIAN

SEA

SICILY

SEA

SYRACUSE

11

Italy

After leaving Malta, Paul's ship next docked at Syracuse, about 100 miles away. Located on the east coast of Sicily, Syracuse was the principal city of the island. From Syracuse the apostle sailed northeastward to Rhegium (modern Reggio) on the toe of the Italian boot. Near there the passage between Sicily and Italy was only about 1 mile wide in ancient times. The ship lay becalmed in the harbor of Rhegium for a day, waiting for a south wind so that it could sail to Puteoli. The Rhegium to Puteoli run, a distance of 180 miles, probably took about 26 hours. Puteoli was the great commercial port of Italy, located on what is now called the Bay of Naples.

Puteoli became the chief port of Rome, though it was about 150 miles away. It won that distinction because of the safety of its harbor and the inhospitality of the coast near Rome. Although the Emperor Claudius (A.D. 41-54) created an artificial harbor at Ostia (near Rome), Puteoli's trade had not markedly declined in the days of Nero, when Paul came through. Puteoli had an excellent port. It was well-sheltered by its natural situation and was further protected by an extensive mole or pier thrown out into the bay at least 418 yards. From Puteoli, the apostolic company took the tomb-lined Via Consularis to Capua (20 miles away), where it joined the main line of the Appian Way. The distance from Puteoli to Rome was 142 English miles, a journey of 5 days for an active traveler. Paul was now on his way to Rome, the city that had for some 200 years dominated the Mediterranean world and was by far the largest metropolis of Italy.

Slashing diagonally across the center of the Mediterranean, Italy is strategically located for control of that sea. After she had annexed Sicily, Italy was in a position to dominate the east-west sea lanes. Roman arms made the Mediterranean a Roman lake, surrounded on all sides by Roman territory. The sea (some 2,300 miles from east to west), not the lands around it, was the center of the empire. The sea routes were the arteries through which the trade of the empire flowed. Mediterranean ports were the chief cities of the Roman world.

Whereas Italy was strategically located for controlling the Mediterranean, Rome was strategically located for controlling the peninsula of Italy. Situated in the center of the peninsula, she could meet her enemies one by one and could prevent them from effectively uniting against her. If such a combination should be formed, she could move against it with the advantage of a central base and short lines of communication. Early in her career of expansion, Rome developed the practice of building military roads to all parts of her domain. Moreover, Rome was located at the lowest point of the Tiber River where firm abutments for a bridge could be found. So Rome controlled the main line of communication along the western and more populous side of the peninsula. As is well known, Rome was built on seven hills.[1] None of them exceeded 200 feet above sea level, but they rose for the most part in steep slopes above the surrounding valleys and at some points formed sheer cliffs towering over these valleys. The Tiber flowed past and later through the city and was navigable for the 15-mile distance between the coast and the capital. Ships docked at the foot of the Aventine Hill. Rome's days as a leading center of trade did not come until the reign of Claudius, however, when her port of Ostia was developed. Even then most of the trade consisted of imports.

When Paul came to Rome during the days of Nero, it was a large city that may have approximated a million inhabitants. The center of activity was the Roman Forum and the adjacent new forums of Julius and Augustus Caesar, located between the Capitoline and Palatine hills. In them stood the Senate, numerous temples, and judicial and commercial structures. Between the Palatine and the Aventine sprawled the

---

1. Capitoline, Palatine, Aventine, Caelian, Esquiline, Viminal, Quirinal. Eventually it expanded onto other hills, including the Pincio and Janiculum.

Circus Maximus, the huge race track and entertainment center with seating for perhaps 200,000. Atop the Palatine stood Nero's palace and west of the Tiber in the Vaticanus region were Nero's circus and gardens. The Colosseum was not built until A.D. 80, some 15 years after Paul's death.

The area of Italy is composed of some 90,000 square miles, a little less than that of Oregon. It divides into two regions: the continental on the north and the peninsular on the south. The northern region is some 320 miles east and west and about 70 miles north and south; the boot-shaped peninsula stretches some 700 miles toward the continent of Africa and is never more than 125 miles wide. In the toe and heel of the "boot," the peninsula is only about 25 miles wide.

Mountains

Mountains dominate much of the landscape of Italy. The Alps form an irregular 1,200-mile arc across the north. While they rise rather abruptly on the Italian side and impede expansion, they slope more gently on the European side and did not prevent migration into Italy. The Apennines extend the full length of the peninsula in a bow-shaped range about 800 miles long and 25 to 85 miles wide. Since the average height of these mountains is only about 4,000 feet, and since the passes through them are not generally difficult, they did not pose the problem to the unification of the country that the mountains of Greece did. The Apennines approach the Adriatic Sea, permitting little more than a coastal road in many places along the eastern coast, while on the west they leave room for arable lands that are carved up into plains by spurs extending from the main Apennine Range. Therefore Italy faced west. Because she did, the flow of culture from the more highly developed civilizations of the East was slowed in its journey to her shores. Along the west coast of the peninsula, both north and south of the Tiber and on adjacent islands, are extinct volcanoes. Active since ancient times have been Vesuvius, Stromboli, and Etna.

Rivers

Several sizable rivers originate in the mountains of Italy. Longest of these is the Po, which rises in the western Alps and flows eastward for

360 miles to the Adriatic Sea. This alone of the Italian rivers can be classified as navigable. Along the Adriatic, rushing mountain torrents punctuate the rocky coastline. Flowing into the Tyrrhenian Sea and navigable by small craft are the Volturno, the Liri (Liris), the Tiber, and the Arno rivers. Not only did the rivers of Italy fail to give the desired highway to much of the land, but they presented a special health problem. The sill at the Straits of Gibraltar breaks the force of the ocean tides flowing into the Mediterranean; and this lack of brisk tidal movement prevents a daily scouring of the coasts. Consequently, the accumulation of silt at the river mouths creates marshy areas that serve as breeding spots for malarial mosquitos. Both in ancient and modern times Italy has suffered much from this dread disease.

Harbors

As can be readily seen, the silting up of the river mouths prevented Italian rivers from providing much in the way of harbor facilities. So extensive was this silting that, in the days of the Emperor Claudius (A.D. 41-54), it was necessary to make a new cut for the discharge of the Tiber into the sea. Moreover, throughout a coastal length of over 2,000 miles, Italy has few deep bays or good harbors. Almost all of those that do exist are located on the southern and western shores. The chief harbor on the Adriatic was Brundisium, far down on the heel of Italy; to the south, Tarentum (Taranto) on the gulf of that name; on the west, Puteoli (Pozzuoli) on the Bay of Naples. Genoa and Lunae Portus (La Spezia) became important only in late Roman times. Ostia, which assumed importance as the port of Rome during the first century A.D., was a man-made harbor.

Climate

The climate of Italy differs in the northern and southern regions. The Po Valley climate is similar to the continental climate of central Europe, with marked differences between summer and winter temperatures, and clearly defined periods of spring and fall. There are frequent winter snows, copious spring and fall rains, and moderate rains in the summer. The climate of peninsular Italy conforms more closely to the Mediterranean type, with boisterous rain-washed winters—during which the Apennines lie heavily mantled with snow—and summers of deficient rain. On much of the peninsula the drought extends for 3 or 4 months; at Rome, 2 months. Land and sea breezes temper the heat. In general, the climate of the west and south coasts is subtropical. It is now generally believed that the climate of Italy has not changed since classical times.

Plains

A further word must be said about the plains of Italy. The large, level, and fertile Po Valley was the best grainland, but it was never an important source of supply for Rome. Since bulky goods had to be transported by water, Romans found it cheaper to obtain their food supply from a closer source. The distance from the mouth of the Po to Rome is longer than that from Sicily or North Africa and very little shorter than that from Egypt. Etruria is rough and broken by stone and better suited for pasture than for cultivation. Latium and Campania are small; their rich but shallow surface soil was soon exhausted, leaving a volcanic subsoil better for orchards and vineyards than for grain. But Campania was for long the chief granary of peninsular Italy and produced large amounts of fruits and vegetables.

Resources

Italy's primary source of wealth was always agricultural and pastoral. As some of the grain-producing soil became exhausted, farmers turned more to viniculture and pastoral pursuits. In fact, the name *Italia* was derived from the Oscan word *vitelliu*, meaning "calf-land." There were also notable mineral resources in ancient times, especially the copper and iron beds of Etruria and Elba. The marble quarries of Carrara in Liguria were first exploited in the last days of the Republic. There was limestone for building purposes; the best was travertine from Tibur (Tivoli) near Rome. Large stands of timber still covered the mountainous areas and some of the lowlands in the first centuries of the Christian Era. Italy also had abundant supplies of good clay for pottery, bricks, and tile.

There are biblical indications and extrabiblical evidence that Paul was released from his two-year Roman imprisonment and had the freedom to move about the Mediterranean world to evangelize once more. Very likely he went to France and Spain, as well as to the Greek East, on subsequent preaching missions. But there is so little information on his later activities that Italy may be considered as the western-most of the Bible lands. And we may limit the Bible lands to eleven, if we think of Palestine as a geographical unit instead of politically divided into Israel and Jordan.

Books for Further Study

A book of this sort cannot be produced by a study of a few book-length geographies of the eleven Bible lands discussed here; such books do not exist for many of the Bible lands. Nor are there books that neatly package the geography of all Bible lands in one volume.

A longer work that does describe all the Bible lands is *The Wycliffe Historical Geography of Bible Lands* by Charles F. Pfeiffer and Howard F. Vos (Chicago: Moody, 1967). Books that provide fairly good discussions of several Bible lands are *Biblical Backgrounds* by J. McKee Adams, revised by Joseph A. Callaway (Nashville: Broadman, 1965) and Max Cary's *The Geographic Background of Greek and Roman History* (Oxford: Clarendon, 1949). The latter deals with many lands controlled by the Greeks or Romans around the Mediterranean Sea.

Unfortunately, even most of the standard Bible atlases concentrate on Palestine, to the exclusion of other countries related to the biblical narrative. One of the newer atlases that remedies that situation to a degree is the *Atlas of the Biblical World* by Denis Baly and A. D. Tushingham (New York: World, 1971). Unfortunately also, most of the standard Bible atlases tend to be somewhat liberal in theological orientation. One that is theologically conservative is Charles F. Pfeiffer's *Baker's Bible Atlas* (Grand Rapids: Baker, 1961).

Of course, Palestine comes in for the lion's share of attention in the

119

literature of Bible geography. Especially significant or useful books are Yohanan Aharoni's *The Land of the Bible* (London: Burns & Oates, 1967); Denis Baly's *The Geography of the Bible* (New York: Harper & Row, 1957); Nelson Glueck's *The River Jordan* (Philadelphia: Westminster, 1946); Efraim Orni and Elisha Efrat's *Geography of Israel*, 3d rev. ed. (Jerusalem: Israel U., 1971); and the magnificent *Atlas of Israel*, produced by a number of Israeli scholars (Amsterdam: Elsevier, 1970). Other especially useful atlases include: Yohanan Aharoni and Michael Avi-Yonah's *Macmillan Bible Atlas* (New York: Macmillan, 1968); Luc Grollenberg's *Atlas of the Bible* (London: Nelson, 1956); Herbert G. May and others' *Oxford Bible Atlas* (New York: Oxford U., 1962); and G. E. Wright and F. W. Filson's *Westminster Historical Atlas to the Bible*, rev. ed. (Philadelphia: Westminster, 1956).

For the study of Mesopotamia in ancient times, Martin A. Beek's *Altas of Mesopotamia* (London: Nelson & Sons, 1962) is extremely important. Hermann Kees's *Ancient Egypt* (Chicago: U. of Chicago, 1961) is one of the most useful works on Egyptian geography. But John Baines and Jaromir Malek have produced the definitive *Altlas of Ancient Egypt* (New York: Facts on File, 1980). Sir William Ramsay's old work *The Historical Geography of Asia Minor* (London: John Murray, 1890; reprint, New York: Cooper Square, 1972) is still very important for an understanding of Asia Minor. *A Dictionary of Greek and Roman Geography*, in two volumes, edited by William Smith (London: John Murray, 1873; reprint, New York: AMS Press, 1966), gives an extraordinary amount of geographical detail for the study of individual Greek and Roman sites. The new atlases describing ancient Greece and Rome are Peter Levi's *Atlas of the Greek World* (New York: Facts on File, 1980) and Tim Cornell and John Matthews's *Atlas of the Roman World* (New York: Facts on File, 1982).

It seems that the only way one can get a true grasp of the geography of all the Bible lands is to note geographical references in a host of ancient and modern geography and history books, archaeological reports, art books, and other specialized treatments, as well as through extensive travel in the Bible lands; and that is how this book has been put together.

Moody Press, a ministry of the Moody Bible Institute, is designed for education, evangelization, and edification. If we may assist you in knowing more about Christ and the Christian life, please write us without obligation: Moody Press, c/o MLM, Chicago, Illinois 60610.